THE YIELDING WARRIOR

DISCOVERING THE SECRET PATH TO UNLEASHING YOUR TRUE POTENTIAL

JEFF PATTERSON

CONTENTS

Introduction   vii

PART I
UNDERSTANDING YIELDING

1. What is Yielding and Where Is It Useful?   3
2. Physical Yielding   17
3. Mental Yielding   33
4. Emotional Yielding   57

PART II
LIFESTYLE APPLICATIONS

5. Learning to Use Yielding Skills in Communication   79
6. Yielding to Intuition – Listening Within   95
7. The Reality behind Meditative Insight   109
8. Tai Chi Chuan and Qigong Theory   125

PART III
STRATEGIES FOR DEVELOPING A PERSONALIZED YIELDING PRACTICE

9. Meditations That Develop Higher Levels of Yielding   143
10. Tapping into Qi and Jin   171
11. Standing and Moving Meditations   189

Conclusion   207
Appendix A: The Five Element / Phase Theory and Yielding   213
Resources   247
Acknowledgments   249
About the Author   251
Thank You   255

Difference Press

Washington, DC, USA

Copyright © Jeff Patterson, 2023

ISBN 978-1-7363200-0-6

All rights reserved. No part of this book may be reproduced in any form without permission in writing from the author. Reviewers may quote brief passages in reviews.

Published 2023

DISCLAIMER

No part of this publication may be reproduced or transmitted in any form or by any means, mechanical or electronic, including photocopying or recording, or by any information storage and retrieval system, or transmitted by email without permission in writing from the author.

Neither the author nor the publisher assumes any responsibility for errors, omissions, or contrary interpretations of the subject matter herein. Any perceived slight of any individual or organization is purely unintentional.

Brand and product names are trademarks or registered trademarks of their respective owners.

Cover design: Jennifer Stimson

First, I would like to thank my family for being supportive of me following my passion. My wife, Kimberly, for always being there when I needed her. My children, Lucas and Sofia, for keeping the light shining bright in my life. They make me want to do everything better and help me to see things I may otherwise have passed over.

Second, I would like to thank Susan Stoner for all of her help content editing this book. If it was not for her talent and generosity, this book would not have become what it is today.

Lastly, thank you to all of my students for your support over the years.

INTRODUCTION

Yielding is an elusive concept, frequently manifesting in ways that words are inadequate to describe. Often the workings of yielding are invisible and seem mystical. The warrior traditions define yielding as the mental and physical act of identifying and using the least amount of resistance necessary to accomplish the desired outcome. Yielding does not mean giving up – quite the contrary. People skilled in yielding have heightened their internal and external awareness to such a degree that they can transform ineffective resistance into a response capable of achieving their end goal with the least amount of effort.

Yielding awareness is a powerful concept that is, to some degree, incorporated in every martial arts tradition, including even the more aggressive martial arts like Muay Thai and Western Boxing. Every high-level practitioner of martial arts understands and uses yielding awareness. What I came to discover, during my thirty-six years of study and teaching, is that yielding awareness is a skill that can be just as powerful and effective in everyday life as it is in martial arts. Moreover, I've seen that yielding is a skill anyone can acquire by using the simple, practical techniques described in this book.

I found that my yielding awareness deepened and evolved over time and with practice. How this enhanced awareness is acquired is unique to every individual, though yielding's positive outcomes are universal. Over the years, I witnessed thousands of my students in both group classes and private classes at my academy undergo yielding's transformative process.

I found a variety of techniques and stratagems to enhance my yielding awareness. What was surprising and rewarding was the discovery, along the way, that yielding's gifts are applicable to every aspect of my life as a student, teacher, friend, husband, father, businessman, citizen, and martial artist. I also came to understand that yielding's benefits increase and reveal themselves only with time and practice – there is no "quick fix." A classic parable illustrates this point:

> There was an elderly master who lived in a remote village nestled in the mountains. He had a reputation for being able to transform ordinary rocks into gold, and thus was widely recognized by the villagers. Many individuals would bring him rocks, hoping that he would work his magic and turn them into gold. Despite being inundated with requests, the old master was always gracious and willing to assist.
>
> One day a young boy from the village came to visit him. He asked, "Honorable master, I understand that you can change an ordinary rock into a piece of gold. Is this true?"
>
> The old master answered, "Yes, it is. If you would like, I would be happy to give you a piece of gold like I do for all the others. Go outside and bring me a rock and I will change it to gold for you."
>
> "Oh no, honorable master," said the boy. "That would be very kind, but I do not want a piece of gold. What I would like to learn from you is how to change the rocks into gold."
>
> The master was impressed that the boy was different than everyone else, and he smiled. The young boy was

smart enough to realize that if the master gave him a piece of gold, it would soon be gone. However, if he understood the process, he would have enough gold to last for the rest of his life.

When you are learning something, what do you aim for? Do you just want quick results, or do you look for a way to get the best results in the long run? When you see flowers or eat fruit, what do you think of? Do you just notice how beautiful the flowers are or how sweet the fruit is, or do you think of how you can grow them?

Stories like these have always intrigued me. Often, they will leave you with a thought or inspire you to see something from a new angle. I have been practicing the martial and meditative arts for over thirty-six years, and I have come across many teachers along the way who use stories such as this one. (I use the term *martial arts* to mean any combat art form, such as Muay Thai, Jiu-Jitsu, Tai Chi Chuan, Western Boxing, or Eskrima.) What's special about this form of learning is often the story will connect with you on a personal level while at the same time teach you valuable life lessons.

In this book, we are going to break down the concept of yielding. You will learn how to use this practice in every area of your life. It will help you become a better friend, father, mother, brother, sister, athlete, martial artist, musician, writer, artist, or anything else in life you desire. You will learn proven strategies that have been studied for thousands of years. Some works you may be familiar with include Laozi's Tao Te Ching (also known as the Dao De Jing), Sun Tzu's *The Art of War*, *The 48 Laws of Power* by Robert Greene, and *The Psychology of Winning* by Denis Waitley. All of these books and the lessons within touch on the idea of yielding.

I started practicing martial arts in my late teens and was struck by the idea that there's more to being successful in combat than just strength and power. After a couple of years of practice, I met an instructor who was a successful boxing coach. At that time, boxing was my favorite martial art. I was young; I loved the pace, the intensity, and the fact that boxing has many layers of strategy. If you are not present and focused in the ring, you will either learn to be, or quit altogether. I asked this coach if he would teach me. He told me he would consider it, but first, he asked me to write him a letter telling him why I wanted to train and to list what my goals were. I wanted to impress him so that he would take me on as a student. This was the first time I considered my martial arts training beyond simply improving fighting skills and having fun.

He took me on as a new student, and I came to him with an empty cup. We had been training for only about two to three weeks when he told me, "If you want to be the best boxer you can be, you should start practicing Tai Chi Chuan (Tai Chi) and meditation." I was about nineteen years old. The only thing I knew about Tai Chi was that old people practiced it in the park downtown. I remember thinking, *I just want to get better at martial arts, but is Tai Chi really something I want to do?*

I had a lot of respect for him as a teacher, so I did not want to tell him I would do it and then only give it half of my energy. If I was going to take on the practice, I would approach it like my boxing and seriously commit to the training. So, after a couple of weeks of consideration, I told him I would like to add Tai Chi and meditation to my practice. This was the true beginning of my martial arts career.

In my first year of practicing the meditative arts, I was disciplined, practicing for at least an hour and a half every day. I noticed some changes but did not know if it was helping me advance in the ring. After eight months of practice, my teacher had only shown me the first few movements of the Yang Tai Chi Chuan form. I began feeling like I was being held back. Then one day things shifted. My ninety-minute sessions seemed to go by in fifteen minutes, and my body made connections I never knew were there. I was able to effectively spar with some of the pros in the boxing gym. My increased focus made me feel like things were happening the way I intended and with less effort.

Only once these things started coming together did he teach me the final 75 percent of the Tai Chi form in about two weeks. Again, I spent eight-plus months working on the first 25 percent and learned the rest in two weeks. I didn't totally understand the process as it unfolded, but I could see it was working.

While I still wanted to push forward with my martial training, I found that my desire to dive deeper into the meditative arts was also growing. After another two years, I was practicing two and a half hours every day, and I started seeking out different teachers around the world.

As I discovered my passion for the martial and meditative arts, I also realized I wanted to share what I was learning with others. Twenty-eight years later, the academy I cofounded is still going strong. We have had thousands of students come through the academy and I have been extremely fortunate to be around so many amazing individuals. Some of our students have been with us for over twenty-five years, and I feel like they are part of my family. Being a student and a teacher of these arts is a special gift. I have learned many things about meditation and teaching from the students here at the academy. Each student comes from a unique background and wants different things out of their training. People approach the meditative arts for many different reasons. Listed here are the five primary directions of the practice, although it is important to note that during your training, you will frequently concentrate on two or even three of these areas. Tai Chi and Qigong training uses five different approaches, all of which are touched on in these pages:

1. Martial Arts
2. Therapeutic
3. Eastern Medical
4. Philosophical
5. Spiritual/Meditative

Within these five approaches, the student uses three methods to cultivate skills in each: ritual, active, and philosophical. When starting a meditation practice, you want to integrate all three. Let's look at how that integration occurs.

Ritual Method

Ritual based practice is the most important and includes standing meditation, sitting meditations, Tai Chi Chuan forms, Qigong sets, yoga, and walking meditation. I always tell new students that they should commit to at least fifteen to twenty minutes of a ritual practice a day. Consistency is key to any meditative art. Meditation is not a hobby that you do once or twice a week but rather a way of life.

I get it; finding the time and energy to establish that consistency is hard. After thirty years of teaching meditative arts to over twenty thousand students I have heard thousands of excuses. It can be rejuvenating to take five minutes a day for a few deep breaths, but the truth is that you will only achieve the full extent of meditation's benefits – about which you've probably read the studies and seen the brain scans – with consistent effort over time.

As one of my teachers once said, "Consistency is key in spiritual practice. It is natural to feel anxious when progress seems minimal in our day-to-day endeavors, yet we must exercise patience until the results of our accumulated efforts become visible. Self-cultivation entails steady and gradual advancement. Ceasing prematurely would have more adverse consequences than not embarking on the journey at all."

If you are considering starting a meditative practice or want to make adjustments to one you currently have, devote twenty minutes a day to it for one year. The students who follow this advice end up seeing so many benefits they always continue on long beyond that first year.

One wise but unattributed proverb says, "You should meditate for twenty minutes a day, unless you are too busy, then you should meditate for an hour." So many people think they do not have the time for a meditation practice when really, we don't have enough time *not* to build one and reap its rewards. One of the great things about the meditative arts is that you do not need to spend two hours a day or retire to a cave in the mountains to get benefits from your practice. By doing your twenty-minute session and implementing active practices into your day, you can receive many benefits from meditation. If you do not already have someone to help you build a meditation practice, seek out a qualified teacher. If there are no options in your area, please check out The Yielding Warrior online program at: https://portlandtaichiacademy.com/online-training/

Active Methods

Active methods are a bit easier to implement, especially for folks who find it hard to escape the mutterings of their minds when they try to quiet it down. They can be done in as little as thirty seconds and include movement practices, breath work, energetic circulations, and mindset training. Meditation is a way of life, and active practices will allow you to integrate these rituals into your day, build momentum, and get the most out of your training. The great thing about active practices is that they help maintain your physical and mental balance throughout the day, leading to reduced stress and more energy to focus on what is important to you.

Philosophical Methods

Lastly, the philosophical method can be incorporated into both ritual and active-based methods of training. Philosophical training expands your mind and opens it up to possibilities that are outside your customary perspective. It also reinforces positive attributes to build your confidence and understand situations through more than one lens. It can be as simple as employing the inner smile, which we will get into later, or memorizing parts of the Dao Te Jing to become more strategic in your thinking.

Weeding through all the resources out there can be a daunting task, so we're going to break them down to be as evidence-based and digestible as possible. Twenty years ago, I had a gentleman come into the academy who wanted to get his teaching certification in Tai Chi Chuan. He had been practicing for about ten years and told me that he had a disciplined training schedule that included at least two and a half hours per day of Tai Chi. I was looking forward to training with him and getting to know him.

When I asked him where he learned his Tai Chi, he said from David Carradine videos. I have nothing against Mr. Carradine, but I found myself skeptical. Sure enough, during his first few sessions, the level of his practice was not very advanced, to say the least. He became discouraged. Here he had spent ten years and thousands of hours training in Tai Chi Chuan, yet he was seeing students at the academy who had only been training for a year who had far surpassed him. He only lasted a few weeks before moving on. Looking back, I wonder how far along he would have been after those ten years had he met a good instructor early on in his training.

My point is that you need a teacher. It is said that "a slight error can cause a thousand-mile divergence." Historically, in the martial arts, there were two kinds of students – the general population and the inner circle. The general students were often accepted for their money or to test their seriousness. They were taught only forms and a minimum of applications and theory. Once a student had spent a sufficient amount of time and proved their loyalty, they were accepted to the inner circle and taught the deeper aspects of the art.

Today, it is often much easier to learn many of these applications through numerous publications, videos, and other sources. This is good and bad. There is so much information out there that it is next to impossible for the beginner student to know what has value and what is a waste of time. (If you do not have access to quality instruction, you might consider checking out https://portlandtaichiacademy.com/online-training/. This is an online program that has a lifetime's worth of lessons to help you build a meditative practice that fits your lifestyle. Start by developing a solid, ritual-based practice that incorporates active and philosophical elements you can use throughout your day.)

Before choosing a method, determine what you want to accomplish. Not all meditation approaches yield the same results; some are designed to reduce stress and make you more centered, others build energy and expand awareness. As I look back over the last thirty-six years of learning and teaching these arts, there have been many directions of potential focus. While I find most of these areas of focus to have a deep value, it is the art of yielding that has always intrigued me most. It remains an endless source of inspiration. An example of the power inherent in yielding is outlined in the following story, the origins of which are lost in the sands of time:

> Back in the Qing Dynasty, there was a young boy whose parents were killed during the invasion of his village. He decided to seek out the head priest of the Shaolin Temple.
>
> When he arrived at the temple, he asked to see the head priest and one of the monks took the boy to where the head priest was meditating. The boy did not want to disturb him, so he waited patiently. When the head priest was finished, the boy kneeled down on the floor and asked: "Honorable Sifu, will you accept me as your Kung Fu apprentice? I will be loyal, respectful, and follow your guidance to become the best student I can be."
>
> The head priest acknowledged the boy but wanted to give him a test before he would accept him as one of his disciples. He said: "Young man, I would like to teach you Kung Fu, but I must leave the temple for one year to travel around the country teaching meditation. Could you do something for me while I am away?" In his excitement the

boy said: "Of course, honorable Sifu! What would you like me to do for you while you are away?"

The head priest took the boy for a walk in the forest and pointed to a huge Dawn Redwood tree. He said: "I have always wanted a beautiful carving of the Buddha. Could you chop this tree down and carve a Buddha for me?" The young lad replied with enthusiasm: "Yes, Sifu! I will have the Buddha ready for you when you return."

Later that week, the head priest departed, leaving the boy to live at the temple with the rest of the monks. Soon after his departure the young man chopped down the tree and made preparations to begin working on the Buddha.

The boy wanted to make the perfect Buddha to impress the head priest. He worked long hours, day and night, carefully carving the best he could.

A year later, the head priest returned to the temple from his teaching. The boy was excited and could not wait to show the priest his work. He took the head priest to the Buddha, which was five feet tall and beautiful. He thought for sure the head priest would now accept him as a disciple.

The head priest could tell the boy had sincerely done his best. However, he wanted to give the boy another test. He said: "Young man, you have done well. But it is too big for me. I was hoping for something smaller. I have to leave the temple for another year, will you make this Buddha smaller for me while I am gone?"

The boy tried to hide his frustration and disappointment. He thought for sure when the head priest saw his work he would be accepted as a student. But his desire to learn Kung Fu was strong so he told the head priest: "Yes, Sifu. I will carve a smaller Buddha for you." Even though the boy agreed, the head priest could see the boy was frustrated.

Later that month, the head priest left for another year and the boy began working on the smaller Buddha. Because he was unhappy and disappointed, he had to force himself to work, not putting his heart in to his labors. Six months passed, and he had carved an ugly Buddha.

Then he realized that he was depressed and could not work on the Buddha when he was upset, so he stopped working. Time passed and the return of the head priest was approaching. His chance of becoming a student did not look promising.

One day as he was walking in the forest, he had a realization and said to himself: "If making this Buddha is my path to my life's dreams of becoming a Kung Fu master, I will make it good and enjoy the process."

The change in attitude not only made him happy again, but he discovered his focus and patience was stronger than ever. He worked late into the night every day. His enthusiasm was stronger than ever before, and he completed his happy, refined Buddha.

As soon as the head priest returned, the boy came to present him with his new, improved smaller Buddha. The new Buddha was about two feet tall, smiling and beautiful. The head priest was very impressed. He knew that the boy had accomplished one of life's hardest challenges: conquering himself.

However, he wanted to give the boy one final test. He said: "This is a beautiful Buddha and your work is impressive. But it is still a bit too big for me. Soon I will leave the temple again for another year of teaching. While I am away, will you make it smaller?"

This time the boy was not disappointed at all. He said: "Of course, Sifu. I will make the Buddha smaller for you." The young man had learned to enjoy the process.

Thus, when the head priest left the boy was excited to begin his work. He used every possible minute to complete the Buddha. His sincerity and maturity began to show life in his work.

The next year when the head priest returned the boy handed him the new Buddha which was only two inches tall. The head priest had never seen a Buddha like it before. He knew now that this young man would be a successful martial artist. After years of hard work and dedication, the young man became one of the most skilled students in the Shaolin Temple.

It was only after the boy had acknowledged and yielded to his frustration and mental defeat that he was able to be at ease and do his best work. This is a standard old-school style of teaching yielding in China. There are many stories of students who were told to practice their standing meditation for three years (or a similar challenge) before they were accepted as students. Often in life we are faced with obstacles that may seem overwhelming; understanding yielding will help put you in the right mental space to approach anything in a strategic way. By learning to guide your mind and emotions, you will often create your masterpiece.

Every person possesses two minds, one grounded in emotions and reactivity, and the other coming from a place of wisdom and sound judgment. Do you recall any instances where you were required to do something but resisted doing it? Your emotional mind was lazy, but your wisdom mind was asking you to perform the task. Who won the battle? You will conquer yourself once you learn to listen to your wisdom mind, leading to success in the future.

Read on to learn how you can use yielding to improve your relationships, life strategies, attitude, work situations, focus, and outlook on life. Yielding will make you more aware and empower your wisdom mind. When we can understand how these mind-conflicts arise, it is easier to adjust and not let negative emotions lead us off track. This higher level of awareness increases your energy and gives you a more accurate and profound experience of reality.

Yielding is an amazing concept. Hopefully, after reading this book, you understand why it is worth your time to apply these lessons to your life. If you do, I am very interested in hearing what lessons you may have learned through your cultivation of these practices. I will be grateful if you check out my Facebook page at https://www.facebook.com/TaichiYielding and let me hear about your thoughts and experiences related to yielding. Thank you.

PART I
UNDERSTANDING YIELDING

1
WHAT IS YIELDING AND WHERE IS IT USEFUL?

General Principles of Yielding

Have you ever heard the old Chinese saying, "Use four ounces to move a thousand pounds?" This is the basic idea behind the concept of yielding. From a martial or physical standpoint, yielding can be difficult to apply but generally easy to understand. One of my teachers once said, "For every thousand internal martial art practitioners, one has a good understanding of yielding. Out of those with a good understanding, only one in a thousand will achieve a high level of yielding." Basically, just one person in a million practitioners develops a high level of yielding. Nevertheless, yielding is not an impossible concept to grasp. There are ideas and applications of the practice that you will be able to implement immediately.

When learning the physical side of yielding, it is important to have a partner and to both be clear on the mutual objective of the practice. When performing the act of yielding, you will learn to be soft. Being soft means to be relaxed but alert. I always tell my students to imagine they are holding a brand-new infant in their arms. They want to be extremely careful and alert while at the same time being gentle and soft so as to not injure the infant.

Without the softness, it is impossible to detect and respond to the subtle changes in both yourself and your training partner. Once you are soft, you will begin to notice when you are off-balance or tight, when your breath becomes choppy, and when your mind becomes distracted. Being able to listen internally to all of these different forms of communication from your body will allow you to start fine-tuning the process.

Once your awareness is increased, and you are more in tune with what you are doing on a physical and mental level, you will be able to sense more of what your training partner is doing. First, you will become more sensitive to their alignment and posture, their softness, their pressure, and their balance. Then you will start to notice the changes in their breath, and at even higher levels, you will sense the moment their intent shifts.

With the ability to experience this heightened sensitivity and awareness of yourself and your partner, it will take less effort to guide the movement in the direction you want it to go. When performing the act of yielding, one partner is always yang, or leading the movement, and the other is always yin, or following the movement. This connection of Yin and Yang, where the bodies touch, is the nucleus or Yi (mind) of the movement. Only one of the partners can be in control of this place at any one time.

Yielding in Daily Life

The heightened sensitivity developed through learning yielding can be used in many ways. Imagine you are driving in heavy traffic. First, you begin to wonder if you will arrive at your destination on time. Then you realize there is no chance of being on time and you grow concerned. Your mind begins to race as you think about the consequences of your tardiness. Your breath becomes short and choppy. Suddenly, out of nowhere, someone cuts in front of you; you honk your horn as the other driver, without hesitation, taps his brakes and aggressively waves at you with his middle finger. Now not only are you late, but you are also angry and thinking about how you should respond.

How long does this incident stay with you? Do you let it go and move on? This would clearly be the healthiest choice. On the other hand, does the road rage follow you into the meeting you are late for? When you arrive, the best thing to do is acknowledge your lateness, apologize, and focus on the meeting at hand. Bringing your frustrations with you into the meeting would lead nowhere positive.

If yielding practice has heightened your internal sensitivity, you would be aware of your tension and could change your mental intent immediately, before that distraction's momentum carries you outside your comfort zone. You could also start some deep breathing exercises to help settle your thoughts and keep you focused. Now, when that driver cuts you off, it is easier to smile, not take it personally, and continue on your way.

The ability to effectively yield requires a keen sense of situational awareness. Whenever you walk into a new place, it is a good habit to notice all those present. Is there anyone who looks out of place? Are they shopping, eating food, having a cup of coffee with a friend? Where are the exits? Where are places someone could hide? Is there anything different on your street or a place you regularly attend? These are all things that will help you avoid trouble as well as see opportunity. There are many exercises that you can do to help build your situational awareness.

Law enforcement and the military use the term *360 mindset*. This term is a reminder that the world is not linear. We need to have a focus in all six directions: front, back, left, right, above, and below. The successful resolution of many detective stories hinges on the detective initially making wrong assumptions based on partial information. Only later will he remember the missed clue and put the pieces together.

In real life, maybe you walk into a 7-Eleven and notice someone in the back nervously looking around. You may be seeing something fairly harmless, such as a shoplifter looking to grab a can of beer. But it could also be someone waiting for the right time, or building up enough nerve, to pull out his gun and hold up the store. Whatever the situation, awareness and attention to detail are important for your safety and that of others.

Applying the Principles of Yielding to Personal Interactions

Another way that yielding is used is through our interactions with other people. As I mentioned earlier, in order to reach a high level of physical yielding, we need to expand our internal awareness. As our sensitivity is heightened, and we start to see more of the subtle interactions in the body, an amazing thing starts to happen. Not only is our awareness heightened internally, but we also start to notice things in other people and in the environment that we previously missed, heightening our situational awareness.

One way to use your yielding-developed principles in your everyday life is during interactions with others. If you have increased your awareness and become more sensitive to posture, tone of voice, speaking rhythm changes, and breath, it will be easy to apply the yielding idea. Imagine, for example, that you are having a conversation with your friend, and you bring up an uncomfortable topic. Maybe his breath becomes a bit choppy, and his tone of voice slightly changes. If your awareness is sharp, you can simply shift the conversation before it gets out of hand.

Oftentimes, we do not pick up on these cues, and it can lead to a disagreement or hurt feelings. One of my teachers used to say that "the best love potion is consideration." Now I realize you are not trying to make everyone fall in love with you and sometimes there are uncomfortable things that need to be said. Yielding, however, is a tool that can help you guide the interaction toward a positive outcome.

There are so many other ways to apply yielding in your everyday life. For example, the skills we learn from yielding are useful in work environments. Imagine you really want a promotion and there's a position opening up for which you'd be perfect. Of course, you first want to talk to your boss and express interest in the position. If you want to stand out, though, you may need some preparation. If your situational awareness is keen, you should already know many things about the position. By observing your boss's relationship with the employee leaving the position, you may discover some valuable information. Are they on good terms? Is the employee being fired or promoted? How was their communication? This information will help you present yourself as a desirable candidate, giving you a strong advantage over your competitors.

An additional illustration of employing the heightened awareness facilitated by yielding is by paying attention to detail. When entering a room with numerous thoughts occupying your mind, it is effortless to find yourself in a negative predicament. Frequently, our bodies provide indications of underlying issues before our minds can make the connections. Developing an elevated sense of awareness enables you to harness this ability to your advantage in various situations, whether they involve positive or negative circumstances.

Similarly, if you deal with business negotiations or are in a profession where reading people is essential to high-level success, such as an attorney or police officer, the yielding skill set can be extremely valuable. Certainly, everyone listens when the stakes are high, and they try to pay attention. While some of these skills are instinctual, yielding training will allow one to master these skills, leading to many life benefits that most of the untrained will never see.

Some people may say I am a good skier. I can get down the hill safely and have fun when the conditions are good. If you were to have me race an Olympian freestyle mogul competitor, I would look like an infant trying to crawl. Crawling is what most people are comfortable with when it comes to their level of awareness. The lessons associated with yielding, however, raise that awareness to a much higher level.

The most important skill for developing such sensitivity during interactions with other people is being aware of your own internal status. It is a two-way street. As we begin noting subtle changes in other's reactions, we also become more aware of our own subtle changes. Many times, events will happen in our lives to which we immediately respond with what we feel are appropriate actions. Often, we may get an hour, day, or a week down the line and realize that maybe that was not the best response to that situation. After your response has gained momentum and time has moved on, it may be difficult to go back and change your response or decision. Thus, the interpersonal skills developed through yielding practice enables us to notice our own subtle reactions to a situation before we respond in a way we may regret later on.

Applying the Principles of Yielding in Athletics

Additionally, the principles of yielding can help athletes dramatically elevate their potential. With heightened awareness, the athlete can move in a way that seems effortless. Many famous players like Tom Brady, Serena Williams, Tiger Woods, and Michael Jordan use yielding principles to help them perform at their best. When we get into a deeper discussion of the different kinds of yielding, we will look at how yielding can be used to elevate an athlete's performance.

If you use the yielding strategy, you will have more control over how you live your life and how you relate to yourself and others. You will also find that those around you will enjoy your company more because they will appreciate your thoughtfulness, consideration, and positive company.

Understanding the Similarities of Yielding in Wartime and Noncombat Scenarios

No survey of yielding's benefits could be complete without noting how it's used in warfare. Yielding has been used in combat for thousands of years. This application of yielding manifests as a very old form of military deception, starting with the hands-on clashing of swords all the way to the posturing of leaders trying to influence others to give them what they desire. In warfare, the military commander would feign a retreat or bait a trap for the enemy to walk into. This was a favorite tactic of Sun-Tzu.

The focus of this book, however, is not warfare's yielding strategies. There are many other texts about strategic military yielding if this is something that interests you. The point to make here is that yielding through deception can be effective in noncombat and nonmilitary situations as well.

The appearance of weakness will often bring out an opponent's aggressive nature, causing him to make emotional decisions. Being able to control the front that you present in a threatening situation, whether it be physical, verbal, or mental, is a critical deceptive skill. In the moment, people often respond to what they see or think they understand. If you seem calculating, hostile, and deceptive, they will have their guard up, and it will be difficult to mislead them. It is more important to present a yielding front that does the opposite and disarms their suspicions. The best yielding approach in such a situation is to appear weak or inattentive, leading the opponent to feel superior to you. This will cause them to either ignore you or act aggressively, not fully understanding what they are really moving into. Once they are committed, and it is too late to change tactics, they will learn a hard lesson. They will discover that you are not as weak as they thought and that they are inadequately prepared to counter your response.

Applying the Principles of Yielding to Your Mental State

On the physical level, the idea of yielding is easy to grasp but tricky to apply and master. Yet the mental applications of yielding are sometimes far more elusive. It takes time and practice with the concept to learn how to apply it to everything you do. Once you understand how to apply this practice, you will find your life becoming smoother. You will accomplish more, and you will be able to focus more than ever before.

For example, suppose you are looking at your weekly tasks and they seem overwhelming. Instead of stressing out and dwelling on the obstacles ahead, you could yield by acknowledging that such thoughts are a negative distraction and let go of those thoughts. This yielding will give you more time to focus on what is important. You will become more efficient with your time, and you will accomplish more. Remember that yielding does not mean giving in. Sometimes yielding requires you to position yourself at a different angle, thus putting you in a better position to get the results you desire.

I always try to observe new students so I can determine which areas of practice will resonate well with them and enable them to experience success early on in their training. A former student of mine, John, had a type A personality and was aggressive, forcing things into submission to get the outcome he wanted. He was like this not only with martial arts but also at work and in his personal life. He was successful in business, but he lived with a fairly high level of stress. Usually, when I meet students like John, I know that nine times out of ten, there are only two ways their training will go. They will either excel by diving into it and seeing some great results, or they will move on immediately, thinking it was not the right fit for them. There rarely is a middle ground with this type of student.

Most people, if they do not find something that works for them immediately, move on. What is so important to understand about yielding, as well as any other activity, is that to reach a high level, we need to invest time in building a strong foundation. I was listening to an interview the other day with one of the late Kobe Bryant's coaches. He saw Kobe practicing one day and after the practice said to him, "You are one of the best players in the world, so why is it that you practice such simple drills?"

Kobe looked at him, a friendly smile on his face, and gave the coach a wink, saying very seriously, "Why do you think I am the best player in the world? Because I never get bored with the basics." The upshot of this story is that you need to find a reason to make the basics of whatever you decide to do fun. If you do not enjoy the simplicity of such activities, you will end up wondering why you're unhappy.

People tend to cling to unrealistic expectations, finding it difficult to learn new things. To re-create or improve oneself, one must scrutinize preconceptions and absorb knowledge like the roots of a tree absorb water. I think John's breakthrough came during his third week of training. We were playing Tai Chi push hands and talking about the importance of yielding. John asked me, "Why should I be weak and give my opponent what he wants? It makes me feel like I am losing."

I considered his question and said, "Don't think of it as giving him anything. All you are doing is repositioning yourself so that you are in a better position to attack." When his face lit up, I knew he was intrigued and had opened up to the positive idea behind yielding.

John's experience is an example of how the mental application of yielding is used in martial arts. If your only approach is to either overpower people or butt heads with them, you will be in trouble the minute you come up against someone who is bigger or stronger than you. Understanding and mentally adopting the concept of yielding in martial arts is very powerful because it gives the smaller, weaker person a chance of defeating the stronger, bigger opponent.

One of the famous founders of Brazilian Jiu-Jitsu, Grandmaster Helio Gracie, taught a few of my Jiu-Jitsu instructors. The grandmaster weighed only about 140 pounds. He always used to say, "If you cannot beat someone who is fifty pounds bigger than you, your Jiu-Jitsu skill is not that good." His son, Royce Gracie, weighed in at 170 pounds. It seemed hopeless for Royce Gracie to go up against Ken Shamrock or Dan Severn, since both weighed well over 200 pounds. Yet, he beat them both. This could not have happened without Royce Gracie mentally understanding and physically using the yielding approach.

Physical Manifestations of Yielding

In order to be good at yielding, a lot of things must come into play. First, you need to have a strong root. If you have ever played any contact sports, you know what I mean. There are always some competitors you will come up against who feel like they are fifty pounds bigger than they actually are. This is the result of being rooted. Second, you have to have strong legs because they will allow you to move front, back, left, and right without getting tight and losing your central equilibrium. At the same time, you have to stay relaxed. If your body is stiff, you will be easily moved and lose your balance. Think about how easy it is to pick up a twelve-foot two-by-four versus trying to pick up an uncoiled twelve-foot chain. The board is stiff and easy to lift while the chain is impossible to lift, since part of it dangles on the ground.

Remaining relaxed while strongly rooted enables you to yield without being moved or unbalanced. It makes it difficult for others to manipulate your body and win the advantage. When you are rooted, strong, and relaxed, you are a force to be reckoned with. To take your yielding to the next level of effectiveness, you must also have a smooth, relaxed breath. By having a smooth, relaxed breath, you can move and make connections more fluidly while simultaneously increasing your timing, speed, and coordination. Lastly, if your Yi or mind remains present in the moment, you have achieved the "whole package." Being able to stay in the moment is what will make every beneficial aspect of yielding come together.

Seems like a simple formula, doesn't it? Well, to make all of these things happen on a high level will take you years and years of practice and training. Yes, some people have natural gifts and can achieve these skills faster than others, but no one can master these skills without thousands of hours of focused training. Don't let this challenge scare you away from undertaking the effort. While it may take many years to master these skills, it is a fun journey, and you will experience benefits from every minute you practice.

There are infinite applications of yielding. Having been

involved with the martial arts for over thirty-six years, I have heard many ancient stories about old monks who did amazing things using the art of yielding. Many Chinese fables talk about emperors who sought advice from wise, mystical monks living in the mountains. While some of these may be fictional stories, I believe there are valuable lessons to be found in them, whether embellished or pure fiction. These old masters were not politicians, nor did they have an in-depth understanding of how society functioned. Yet these old masters were so in tune with the art of yielding that when they would hear of a situation or problem, it was easy for them to step back and identify the most strategic, easy path leading to the best possible outcome.

Yielding and the Ancient Philosophers

Lao-Tzu (sometimes called "Lao-Tze" and "Laozi") was a Chinese philosopher believed to be the founder of the philosophical system of Taoism. The Tao Te Ching, a famous text that has been translated into hundreds of languages, is credited to him as its creator. Although he is commonly referred to as Lao-Tzu, this was not his given name. It is an honorific term denoting "Old Teacher" or "Old Man." Lao-Tzu's existence has been widely debated, with some contending that he may not have actually existed as a single person but rather is a composite of several philosophers. In this regard, the historian William Durant wrote, "Lao-Tze, greatest of the pre-Confucian philosophers, was wiser than Teng Shih. He knew the wisdom of silence, and lived, we may be sure, to a ripe old age – though we are not sure that he lived at all." It is widely believed that Lao-Tzu lived in the sixth century BCE, although there is little historical evidence to confirm his existence. According to a story told by Szuma Ch'ien, a young Confucius once visited Lao-Tzu to ask him a question about individuals in Chinese history. Lao-Tzu's response was as follows:

Those about whom you inquire have molded with their bones into dust. Nothing but their words remain. When the hour of the great man has struck, he rises to leadership; but before his time has come, he is hampered in all that he attempts. I have heard that the successful merchant carefully conceals his wealth and acts as though he has nothing – that the great man, though abounding in achievements, is simple in his manners and appearance. Get rid of your pride and your many ambitions, your affectation, and your extravagant aims. Your character gains nothing for all these. This is my advice to you.

Szuma reported that Confucius was deeply impressed by Lao-Tzu and likened him to a majestic dragon of mythological proportions. Confucius took Lao-Tzu's advice to heart. This led him to dedicate himself to philosophy, concentrating more on his internal wealth than on his outward displays of affluence. This story, while considered fictional, exemplifies the high esteem accorded Lao-Tzu. Regardless of whether Lao-Tzu was an actual or fictional person, there is no denying that he influenced some of the greatest philosophers of China and the world.

There is yet another story one of my Qigong teachers liked to tell about Lao-Tzu. This tale goes as follows:

Lao-Tzu was asked to come to give advice to the Chinese Emperor. The Emperor asked question after question and was very impressed with Lao-Tzu's knowledge and sage advice. Lao-Tzu grew tired and was ready to leave. He wanted to return to the mountains to retire and live the remainder of his years in meditation. Despite the Emperor's reluctance to let him go, Lao Tzu left the kingdom of Zhou and began his journey.

Lao-Tzu reached a river, but it was getting too late to cross it, so he decided to rest for the evening and resume his journey in the morning. Back in the city, however, the Emperor realized he had many more questions he needed to ask the wise old sage. So, he sent his men to ask that Lao-Tzu return.

When the Emperor's men reached Lao-Tzu, they relayed the request, but the sage was not willing to change his plans. So, he told them that he would write down everything the Emperor needed to know. He stayed up all night and wrote all eighty-one chapters of the Tao Te Ching.

Whether this is the accurate depiction of actual events or not, the Tao Te Ching has been studied for centuries. It is a book that has many insights into life and the positive applications of yielding.

Many times, throughout my career, people have asked me, "Why do you practice meditation and Tai Chi?" There are so many benefits of the practice that I could talk for days on the subject. Still, my response is short and sweet: "If the only benefit of meditation and Tai Chi was yielding, it would be enough to compel me to do the practice."

In the following chapters, we will dive deeper into the practice of yielding and learn, in greater detail, how to use this practice to improve any area of your life, including relationships, career, family, friends, creativity, and athletics. The hope is that after reading the specifics you will be inspired by this concept and encouraged to implement yielding skills into every aspect of your life.

2

PHYSICAL YIELDING

If you are a sports fan, I am sure you have a few athletes you highly admire for their unique skill set. Some are like bulls: they use their power and athletic ability to drive through the line or to get past the defender. Others are like spiders: they set their traps and wait for the opportunity to attack. Some are technicians: they know every play and perform with textbook precision. While all of these skills are valuable on a championship team, not every athlete can be so easily defined. Some seem to have a mystical aura about them, and it's hard to put a finger on why they are so great. When it comes to the best of the best – think Michael Jordan, Tom Brady, Willie Mays, Muhammad Ali, Mia Hamm, Rickson Gracie, Simone Biles, and Tiger Woods – they all have a certain mystique. Part of that magic is their mastery of the fine art of yielding – meaning that they are acutely aware of their own internal strengths, weaknesses, and reactions. They are also able to discern and counter those same characteristics in their opponents.

So how does this translate into the actions of stellar athletes? Let's look at a few examples. Yielding is an area of athletic performance that most people do not see or understand among these elite players. But it is from watching them that we can learn a lot about high-level yielding in action.

Basketball

I always love watching the basketball finals. These are high-speed games with athletes who have multiple physical skills. When you watch someone like Michael Jordan play, it is difficult not to be amazed at how he can do what he does. He has an ability to foresee actions in advance and even create unexpected opportunities. His ability to anticipate movement allows him to move through a wall of defenders, frequently making them look like they are amateurs. While no doubt this ability comes from thousands and thousands of focused hours of practicing, at its core, his art demonstrates he has incorporated an extreme amount of yielding into his play.

There are elements of yielding at many levels when a player hits the court. Let's look at a few. First, when a player understands the opponent's game strategy, that player will recognize what intentions are being signaled when the opponent adopts a specific formation. So, as the player's team is bringing the ball down the court and recognizes the opponent's choice of formation, the player's team can react with offensive patterns and points of attack to counter the opponent's defense. In sum, what this situation teaches is the idea that knowing your options and those of others allows you to choose the most effective approach to achieving the desired outcome.

There is a second aspect to this situational awareness that can take you beyond defense into the realm of turning your opponents' intent against them. If you anticipate the thrust of their next actions, you can use the power of their intent to deflect and counterattack. For example, in Tai Chi, a relaxed yielding twist of the waist to counter an opponent's aggressive thrust immediately transforms into a way to throw them off balance while positioning yourself for a devastating, close-in punch. This example demonstrates physical yielding at its best, showing how it is both flexible and dynamic within the moment.

After finishing this book, you will have a deeper understanding of what physical yielding is and have the ability to manifest and see this more subtle athletic skill in yourself and others. At that point, if you go back and watch your favorite athletes' plays you will experience a newfound respect for the underlying yielding strategy that has elevated them to such a high level of performance.

Boxing

Have you ever watched a Muhammed Ali fight? It is amazing how well he could read others. Elite boxers notice every subtle move and can usually tell the intention behind the movement before most people even register something is happening. Fighters need to see every detail of their opponent. When a fighter shifts his weight from one foot to the other, it signals movement or attack. It is easy to watch someone walking down the street and see them shifting their weight from one foot to the other. In a fight, however, this skill needs to be broken down as much as possible.

Imagine standing in a shoulder-width stance and then shifting your weight from one foot to the other. It is easy to feel the shift when you move half of your body weight from your left foot to your right foot. What if the person you are watching only shifts five pounds or two ounces of their weight? Will you see it? Most people will not. Good fighters, those with a cultivated awareness, can often sense their opponent's intention to transfer two ounces of their weight before they actually do so. How is this possible?

A boxer spends hundreds, if not thousands of hours, analyzing his own technique. When training for a big fight, most boxers also study their competitor's techniques. Usually, when two top fighters meet in the ring for the very first time, they have already studied each other's strategies fairly well. In addition to their normal training hours every day in the gym, running, shadowboxing, sparring, and so on, they spend many hours studying their opponents. They analyze every move, feint, and strategy their opponent has made in previous fights, watching their movements over and over. They search for every subtle detail and signaling "tell" that they can use.

They are trying to memorize their technique, and particularly, their opponent's habitual responses and cues that signal when an attack is coming – things like, does his face flinch before he strikes? What is his favorite go-to defense for the left hook? Does he change his guard when he is attacking and defending? As the boxer studies these habits, he will also make note of the evolution of changes the other fighter has undergone in his last few fights. This will allow him to see how his opponent is changing from one fight to the next. With this information, the boxer can then make some rational predictions of what to expect in the coming fight. On fight night, he will take all of this information into the ring as a solid game plan on how best to defeat his opponent.

So, what does all of this fight preparation have to do with yielding? As discussed earlier, in order to be good at yielding, you need to be able to see things as soon or sometimes even before they happen. Studying one's opponents gives a person the tools needed to anticipate the other's moves, thus making it easier to redirect (yield) and come out on the winning side of the exchange.

Remember the earlier discussion that broke down all the skills needed to be good at physical yielding? Skills like being well-rooted, having strong legs so you can change your central equilibrium, keeping your body relaxed, having a smooth and even breath, and keeping your mind present? If you have developed a high level of awareness and use of these yielding skills, you will pick up on subtle changes that most will never see.

Maybe you notice that every time your opponent throws a strike, they inhale deeply before they deliver the blow. Or, when they intend to throw a right-hand punch, their right eye twitches slightly. There are so many subtle signs that fighters learn to pick up on. People will often talk about how Muhammed Ali had amazing speed and timing, and yes, this is true. Often though, they never recognized one of the fundamental skills that make Ali's speed and timing look so impressive – his heightened awareness developed through hundreds of thousands of repetitions and his ability to apply physical yielding. An average amateur boxer will throw approximately a hundred thousand jabs in the three months leading up to a competition. The jab is just one skill he is perfecting. He is also working on footwork, head movement, rear hand, hooks, and uppercuts while building strength through skipping rope, hitting heavy and speed bags, and other such strengthening activities. Have you ever done anything a hundred thousand times? If you have, you will understand how you start to notice the smallest details, and this is where all of the magic begins.

Jiu-Jitsu

Jiu-Jitsu is a highly versatile martial art that offers numerous techniques and approaches. Many practitioners compare it to a game of chess, as it involves strategic thinking and physical execution. The strategy involved in Jiu-Jitsu is what has made me a lifelong practitioner of the art. I have been studying Jiu-Jitsu now for over twenty-eight years and still get excited every time I get on the mat. All high-level practitioners in this game understand the value of yielding.

Master Helio Gracie, one of the founders of Brazilian Jiu-Jitsu, was well known for his soft touch. I have three teachers who personally trained with him, and they all say, "You never realized that you needed to tap out [tapping out is like saying "uncle"; you are letting your partner know you cannot go on and that he has won] until it was too late" – they'd misread his softness. Master Gracie's ability to be soft is what yielding is all about.

As noted in the boxing discussion above, being well-rooted, having a strong lower body so you can change your central equilibrium, being relaxed to increase sensitivity, having a smooth, even breath to help prevent tension, and possessing a present state of mind are all skills essential to physical yielding. These same skills are used in Jiu-Jitsu, but let's look at how they can be used in different ways.

The first skill is having a strong root. When you are standing, this means to be solidly in your feet so that if somebody were to bump into you on the street, they would bounce back or maybe fall over while you would barely move, if at all. In Jiu-Jitsu, you start practicing while on your feet, developing the ability to be rooted. Later, there will be many other positions in your practice as well. Maybe you will be on your back, side, or in a hip-knee-hand tripod or other position. Every position requires a rooted foundation to create power and leverage. In Jiu-Jitsu, you need a strong lower body in order to shift your center equilibrium and prevent getting stuck in an inferior position. If you are on the ground, you need to have developed a strong core, shoulders, and arms as well.

Secondly, and simultaneously, your body must stay relaxed for sensitivity. This is an essential skill if you are going to be relaxed enough to feel an ounce shift of movement. That will make it more difficult for your opponent to overpower you. Breathing is sometimes a challenge in Jiu-Jitsu, like when you find a 250-pound person on top of you. So, you need to learn how to adjust to a posture that will allow you to relax your breath. If you start to feed into the breathing discomfort, you may begin feeling claustrophobic, creating a distraction that leaves an opening for your opponent.

Keeping your mind present will keep you in the moment and enable you to notice all of the subtle changes happening both within yourself and your opponent. When rolling (a Jiu-Jitsu term for freestyle sparring), there are split seconds during the encounter in which to perform a movement. Missed timing will require you to use more muscle or just end up with a missed opportunity.

Policing

There are many situations where yielding principles assist law enforcement. For example, imagine a call comes into 911; there is a report of someone holding a small group hostage at gunpoint. When the police arrive on the scene, they do not always want to burst in the front door trying to surprise the individual. Often, they will signal that they are willing to retreat (yield) by giving the armed gunman something he wants. Simultaneously, they are studying different ways in and out of the building, trying to get a count of how many hostages and gunmen there are. They are analyzing all of the different possible ways the incident can end. As they continue to appear yielding, by showing empathy and aid, they are also repositioning their assets to be in key positions for attack.

Another way officers use yielding relates to gun retention. A police officer must necessarily elevate his or her awareness and pay attention to all details that are presented. Many times, if a suspect is going to try to take a firearm from a police officer, they will glance at the gun in its holster before they make their move. When this happens without more action, it is not an attack, but it is a signal the officer should notice. Immediately, the officer's attention should heighten and adjust his or her position to make it more difficult for the person to grab that gun. If there is more than one glance at the firearm, the officer should verbally address this with the suspect. In most situations, once they realize the officer is alert to a possible gun grab, it will be enough to deflate their confidence in their ability to execute their plan.

Bullying

Yielding can be helpful if you have to deal with a bully. Bullying has garnered significant attention in recent years and deserves our continued focus and consideration. When I was in school, sure, we heard the term *bully* and would often see kids getting bullied, but we were never informed of all the actions that constitute bullying. Nor did we understand the consequences and why it is so important to not get involved with any step of the bullying process.

Today, more kids understand that even just standing around and watching bullying take place is not okay. While there are many tactics we can use to defuse bullying through education and awareness, sometimes it does get physical, and we can feel forced to respond. It is important to educate our teachers, parents, and children on how to deal with bullying. When we understand these tactics and know how to recognize when bulling occurs, we will be more likely to overcome the next bully who comes our way. Some of the yielding techniques we can teach our children are below:

- Avoid the bully or walk away if possible.
- Use humor to defuse the situation. Make a joke: "Hey, Billy, hold on. I don't want you to miss lunch."
- Be assertive and confident. Say, "Get a life. Leave me alone," and then walk away. This is a good defense for girls getting hassled by boys.
- Consider keeping a friend around as bullies may lack the courage to start something when you're with someone else. Therefore, it's important to build friendships and have people in your corner as it decreases the likelihood of becoming a target.

Parents and teachers can help children increase and use their yielding skills in bullying situations in several ways:

- Enrolling your children in a quality martial arts program, teaching them to be assertive and self-confident. It is one of the best ways to build their confidence.
- Teaching kids how to recognize bullying and letting them know what they should do if they witness an act of bullying or end being involved in a specific event.

- Engaging in meaningful communication with children. Ask them about their friends and how their peers treat them. Most kids will never bring up this subject, so we need to actively communicate with them.
- Increasing social opportunities for kids, especially if they are being bullied. Create group situations involving other children so they can bond and build friendships.
- Getting children involved with more activities (sports, clubs, martial arts, or other groups). This is a great way for them to find commonality with other children, building their confidence and their ability to communicate with other kids.
- Making sure they know they can always confide in you. It is important that they understand how to speak up if they witness bullying or are being bullied.

Teaching kids yielding skills will give them more tools and the awareness needed to counter bullies who may cross their path. Below is one example of how yielding skills could be applied in a bullying situation:

Say your son, Lucas, comes home one day and says some kids were picking on him at school. You ask him what happened and find out that this kid, Billy, and his friends were picking on Lucas. Billy was the instigator, and three other kids were standing around laughing when Billy was making fun of your son. After talking with your son, you find out that this was not the first time this happened. Of course, you should notify the teacher so that the school can try to prevent this from happening again.

But it is not always a perfect world and things will not always work out the way we'd like. Ask your son when, where, and how Billy is making fun of him. Are there any consistencies? Does it always happen on the playground, before school, after school, or similar? Is there a focus of the taunting – making fun of his weight, friends, or clothes? If Lucas knows that there are certain topics or places where it is likely he encounters Billy's bullying, he can plan how to avoid them. Maybe it always happens when the kids are at lunch. Lucas could plan how to avoid the encounter. If he notices Billy walking toward him, Lucas could immediately join a group of friends to hang out or play games with. Nurturing friendships with other kids is a great way to deter bullies.

Usually, if Billy and his pals see Lucas involved with other children, they will wait for another opportunity when Lucas seems more vulnerable. You can prepare Lucas by teaching him to have a keen awareness of his surroundings and of others, as well as helping him plan actions he can take to avoid negative encounters. This information will help give him confidence in his ability to anticipate a bullying encounter and know-how to avoid the situation.

However, as I expressed above, things do not always work out perfectly and assertiveness may be needed to redirect the situation. Certainly, it is wise to stop the bully at the first instance, but it is never too late to effectively respond. No one should be allowed to bully just because they can. Unfortunately, it is naive to believe ignoring the first bullying attempt will make the bully go away. If anything, pretending to ignore the bully might make matters worse.

Children should be told they need to put a stop to it the first time, either by being assertive or immediately reporting it to an adult. It is crucial to send the message that bullying behavior will not be accepted or tolerated. The targeted child needs to maintain eye contact and remain calm. Additionally, they should be told to remain themselves in response, to continue wearing their clothes, and using the items a bully has criticized. A child needs to be told he or she should not apologize about who they are or change themselves to make a bully happy.

There is a natural tendency for the targeted person to label themselves a "victim." Humans find it easy to hold on to feelings of injustice, of being wronged. Such feelings can temporarily offer a measure of solace, but those feelings become destructive long-term, leading to stress, depression, and low self-esteem. The solution is not to wallow in the trough of victimization. Instead, the goal should be to analyze the situation and plan how to address it should it arise in the future. This is the yielding approach because it relies on objectively comprehending what has happened both internally and externally. It moves the mind from the reactive and emotional into wise and clear judgment. From that position, it is possible to redirect feelings to the positive and react effectively to similar future situations in a way that will lead to desired outcomes.

However, it's not just children who are bullied. Adults are also bullied in the workplace by their coworkers, supervisors, or managers. The popularity of social networking sites has taken bullying into a new arena. Today, internet sites allow bullies (keyboard warriors or cowards) to target individuals or specific communities that are identifiable by virtue of their ethnicity, religion, race, sexual orientation, or disabilities. In numerous cases, such cyberbullying leads to numerous problems including depression and suicide.

Contrary to what some claim, bullying is not just a disagreement – not even close. Just because you see an individual arguing or finger-pointing at another, it doesn't always mean that they are simply having a "personal" issue. It could mean that one individual is taking advantage of his or her stronger position or the other's weakness to target them for amusement. Bullying is malicious, abusive, and intentionally hurtful. Moreover, even as a bystander, your inaction can make you complicit in the abuse.

It is about time that measures are taken to make bullying a thing of the past. There will always be disagreements and disputes and even practical jokes shared between people. But if one individual is in a position of control or power over the other, then that same behavior can become bullying. Bullying needs to be stopped, and the first step to doing that is to recognize a bully or a bullying incident and refuse to be a part of it, even as a bystander. Experts recommend that, if you see someone being bullied, you should not confront the bully, but instead approach the victim and engage them in an upbeat, positive conversation (like discussing a movie or pretending you are friends) while completely ignoring the presence of the bully. Many times, this tactic will make the bully give up and go away.

Tai Chi Chuan

Another teacher of mine, Master Sam Tam, is a well-respected Tai Chi and Qigong practitioner. He would always say, "With yielding, you can make your enemies become your friends. Without yielding, your friends can become your enemies."

The martial art of Tai Chi Chuan, according to many, originated the concept of yielding in martial arts. Tai Chi push hands is a two-person exercise. Playing Tai Chi push hands heightens your awareness and gives you many insights into physical yielding. When learning Tai Chi, it takes many years to get to a high level of yielding in the practice. Master Tam said, "One person in a thousand people who practice Tai Chi Chuan has a good idea of the concept of yielding. But, only one in a thousand of those is actually good at yielding."

Many practitioners of Tai Chi Chuan find themselves contemplating the philosophy behind this martial art. While practicing push hands alone may not fully prepare you to be a well-rounded fighter, the skills acquired through push hands training can greatly enhance your fighting abilities. The Tai Chi Chuan fighting strategy revolves around the concept of substantial and insubstantial energy, which is applied in every posture and technique. This principle is reflected in the Tai Chi symbol (Yin-Yang symbol), where one side represents lightness and the other side represents darkness, one side represents heaviness and the other side represents weightlessness. In Tai Chi Chuan, when faced with an opponent's attack (substantial), you respond by yielding and neutralizing (becoming insubstantial). This principle guides the practitioner's movements and allows them to effectively respond to their opponent's actions.

When you are able to use this idea, the next step is to simultaneously attack where your opponent is weak. If you were to butt heads with your opponent and attack his strength with yours, you may be able to win if you are strong; this is called "mutual resistance," but it is not the Tai Chi way. You must train so that you automatically respond by yielding to your opponent's attacking force and don't get caught up trying to see who the bigger "meathead" is. As you defend yourself, you can also position yourself for a counterattack or set up your opponent for one.

As stated previously, you offensively attack when the opponent is weak. Just because he appears insubstantial does not mean you should let your guard down, as it could be a trap. Instead, deliver your attack when he is shifting his energy from a substantial state to an insubstantial state, or the other way around. It will be tough for an opponent to turn to defense if you catch them immediately before or right after their attack, and you will have the upper hand, most often winning the exchange.

These substantial and insubstantial energies are controlled by the mind (Yi). When your awareness is heightened and you can sense your opponent's intention, your Yi can change your actions to either attack, yield, or defend. To become successful with this strategy it is important to not use all of your energy. Always conserve some so that you have the ability to easily switch from attack to defense or defense to attack. If you are able to conceal your techniques amid this switch, your opponent will not comprehend your actions. When you appear to be attacking, do not always attack and when you look as if you are withdrawing, do not always withdraw. If your opponent cannot sense your intention, most often you will come out ahead. After many hours of focused practice, your opponent will become unable to discern your actions, whether you are attacking or feigning, resisting or neutralizing, and will be unsure of how you plan to attack. There is an old Tai Chi saying that expresses this idea: "false-false, real-real, real-false, and false-real."

When you fight against an opponent who has highly developed

yielding skills, it is very hard to deliver an attack. When you gather energy to prepare for an attack, your opponent may already sense your intention. In order to be successful, you need to learn how to shorten the amount of time you store the energy before an attack. When you have learned how to shorten the length of time before an attack and can transition easily from substantial to insubstantial, you will be very hard to beat. The Tai Chi classics say:

> Suddenly disappear, suddenly appear. When there is pressure on the left, the left becomes insubstantial; when there is pressure on the right, the right becomes insubstantial. Looking upward it seems to get higher and higher; looking downward it seems to get deeper and deeper. When (the opponent) advances, it seems longer and longer; when (the opponent) retreats, it becomes more and more urgent. A feather cannot be added, and a fly cannot land. The opponent does not know me, but I know the opponent. A hero has no equal because of all of this.

These are some of the ideas on how Tai Chi Chuan or yielding can be used for fighting, but there are many other benefits from doing the practice. It has therapeutic benefits from the slow nature of the movements, and this also makes it very safe. Even if you are just practicing Tai Chi for the many health benefits, playing push hands and studying the yielding applications is fun and you can do it for the rest of your life, well into old age.

Understanding how to use yielding in many of these potential situations can give you enough of an edge to put yourself in a position that is difficult for bullies to attack. If you end up in a situation where bullying is already occurring, you will have the mental skills to divert, redirect, and lead the conversation or situation to a positive outcome. When the event turns physical, experience in yielding will give you the tools to help you gain the advantage and come out unharmed.

As we dive more into the yielding practice, you will understand how having these heightened awareness skills will help you to lead conversations, relationships, and situations in a positive direction. Finally, while you may not be an athlete, find yourself being bullied, or see any direct applications of how you can use yielding at this point, I assure you there are many. Remember to look at these examples as options for your consideration. You will not have the same values or goals that I do, and you will not use yielding the way I do, but if you approach this idea with an open mind, I guarantee you will find ways you can use the yielding practice to positively influence your life.

The Quickie

Next, I want to share a simple technique that you can integrate into your day to help improve your internal awareness. This is great for stress relief. If you are feeling overwhelmed, it will help center you and make you feel grounded. Additionally, this is one of the simplest practices to use. Do this as often as you can. It will increase your awareness, make you more relaxed and present, and help you build a solid foundation for your meditation practice. It can be performed anywhere and with as little as three breaths, though several minutes is preferable. Perform this practice whenever you can and as often as possible.

To begin, start with a natural, slow, smooth breath. As you inhale, take in as much air as you can comfortably. You should not feel that your breath is tight or that you are straining. Then exhale naturally and notice how the tension in your body fades. Every time you exhale, it will feel as if you are sinking into your stance or your seat. As you are breathing, make sure to maintain good alignment and posture. If your posture is not correct, you will not be able to experience a complete, relaxed breath. Continue to observe your posture, your breath, and your overall relaxation. If you can count twenty to fifty breaths, five or more times a day, this will soon become easy and feel natural. It is through regulation of the breath over time that you will begin to naturally breathe this way without any conscious effort. This is what you should strive for, called "regulating without regulating."

As you begin paying attention to your breath, you will notice that every time you are stressed, your breath becomes short or choppy. This feels uncomfortable. When your natural breath is, for the most part, smooth, deep, and relaxed, you will start to notice stressors before they unbalance you. This is one of the great benefits of this practice. Being able to see distractions that send you off-balance will make it easier for you to control your responses and to remain grounded and relaxed even in stressful situations.

3

MENTAL YIELDING

The idea of mental yielding is very inspirational. If we would all use this concept to push our awareness to new levels, the world would be a better place. The previous chapter discussed how yielding's heightened awareness was applied physically and how that heightened awareness helps us see deeper into our physical being. Many examples of physical yielding were offered. Now let's look at how we can use mental yielding and our newfound awareness to take yielding into another dimension – that of our mind.

By noting all of the subtle actions taking place in our bodies, we see things about ourselves that we never noticed before. The same heightened awareness allows us to also see subtle reactions in other people. This is where yielding starts to really get interesting. Mental yielding is an amazing skill. Mastering this skill will lead you to unlimited potential in life. With mental yielding, we start to experience others at a deeper level and access unlimited valuable information.

This chapter looks at how to use mental yielding to read people visually, audibly, and mentally. This will allow you to build more meaningful relationships, find advancement in your career, and achieve higher levels of competence in the areas of competition, group dynamics, tactics, and negotiation.

With yielding it is essential to be able to experience the moment. The purpose of fishing is to catch fish, the purpose of life is to live, which means we need to be present to experience the moment. In other words, you should not get caught up analyzing the world around you and searching for hidden cause and effect relationships of any given situation that you end up standing apart from, for the purpose of interpretation. We do not live conceptually or scientifically defined lives; the essence of the quality of our lives lies in the simplicity of living.

Assume that you are on vacation with your family. You are having an incredible dinner in a nice restaurant listening to your kids tell you stories of the day's events. The scene and the whole experience fill you with assurance, content, and love. Suddenly, however, you think to yourself, *something is missing here! Could this be better? What if we were here at a different time of year or what if we would have gone to that other place instead? How could we make this scenario better?* The problem here is obvious. You can become so wrapped up in thinking of different ways to improve your future that you miss out on all of the joy you are currently experiencing.

Imagine taking your family to Disneyland and everyone is excited. When you get there, you will have a blast. Then you are packing in a rush, yelling at your kids to hurry, and racing to get to the airport; you get frustrated with the service at the parking lot, begin raising your voice at the ticketing agent, and on and on until you finally get to the park. This seems ridiculous, doesn't it? But does it stop there? You think, *Let's hurry up and get to the next ride so we can have fun when we get there.* It is so easy in life to get distracted and lose track of what is truly important. We need to learn to enjoy the journey, not the destination.

The key to a fulfilling life is simply to live it. Avoid interrupting moments of enjoyment by questioning whether you are fully appreciating the experience. Don't strive to observe your own happiness and potentially miss out on the moment. Life truly thrives when it flows naturally through us, without our conscious interference. When we are truly living, we are not aware of the act itself, as life is living through us.

When we start learning to apply mental yielding, many possibilities emerge. By having this heightened sense of awareness, we start to recognize cues from others that give us valuable information. It is a precious skill to see behind the voice and the body language of those with whom you spend time. It allows you to build stronger, more meaningful bonds. Imagine having the ability to make everyone around you feel better. Let's look at how to develop this skill and a few different ways the strategy of mental yielding is applied.

Yielding and the Mind

Your brain is a physical organ. It produces electrical signals at various different frequencies. It has measurable volume and mass. But the mind is more elusive; it is difficult to define. Often, we visualize our mind as residing in our head. Yet it has been proven that our heart, stomach, muscles, and fascia all have the ability to remember. Athletes rely on this phenomenon, calling it "muscle memory." It seems likely that thinking of the mind as residing in our head is to narrow a view of the mind. Rather, it is likely that your mind resides in your entire body.

We all know that your mind has the power to take you into another reality. Imagination has no limits – with it you can readily access the past or foresee the future. It is an infinite resource. Certainly, your mind helps you process information from your body, see things from differing perspectives, and, ultimately, to reach your desired goals.

Science tells us that the brain is composed of approximately one hundred billion neurons. These neurons cycle through periods of firing and resting. The number of times the neurons fire and rest over a particular period of time is called their frequency. The average frequency of an adult's brain, in an awakened state, is approximately twenty cycles per second. This is called the beta wave frequency. At this level of brain activity, you are alert, can hold conversations, and can process information from your surroundings.

The yielding approach teaches how to use different meditation strategies to access two other primary brain wave frequencies: alpha and theta. Learning to condition the mind to be receptive to these frequency waves involves learning and performing meditation exercises. Meditation exercises are similar to how you create memories in your muscles by learning and performing certain physical exercises.

The alpha wave state is slower than beta. Alpha frequencies range from approximately seven to twelve cycles per second. This is the awakened state where creativity, imagination, and intuition are heightened. Many of the meditations you will learn use the alpha state for inspiration and give you greater access to the knowledge within you.

Many of the advanced meditation methods discussed teach how to access an even slower frequency of the brain waves – the theta frequency. You experience the theta wave state every day even if you do not meditate. We all move in and out of this state. You are in a theta state right before you fall asleep and immediately upon awakening. The theta wave state lets you tap into some of your most profound realizations. The mind is capable of higher levels of healing, growth, and insightful learning in the theta state. This is the frequency wave state where it is easiest to connect to your subconscious and realize how to make changes in the material world.

When you meditate, your mind is quieter, less distracted, and less influenced by the habitual perceptual filters which we all use to interpret the world. But while you are in a meditative or dream state, your mind experiences what you see without these influences and therefore you see and experience life more objectively.

You use visualization to recall your past experiences. Yielding will teach you how to exercise and develop skills with visualization, and you are also going to train your imagination. You will use your imaginative ability to create and manifest what you desire. Imagination has many of the same sensing abilities as visualization, but visualization involves referencing something you have already experienced. In contrast, imagination is what you use when you project into your mind's eye what has not yet occurred. With yielding we use both of these skills. Our detailed observations of them help us to direct our present situations.

A visualization study conducted at the University of Chicago offers solid proof of visualization's value in sports. Visualization is a highly effective mental rehearsal technique that is commonly taught in sports, and its power has been supported by numerous studies.

One study was conducted by Dr. Biasiotto, who divided the participants into three groups and tested each group's ability to make successful free throws on a basketball court.

The first group was told to drill free throws for an hour every day. The second group was told to only visualize making successful free throws for one hour per day. The third group was told to forego any further practice or instruction.

After thirty days, Dr. Biasiotto analyzed the groups. The first group's performance improved by 24 percent, while the second group's performance improved by 23 percent, even though they had never physically practiced. The third group, as anticipated, showed no improvement. I do not mention this study because I think you should be lazy and visualize in place of practice. My intent is to drive home the value of both practicing *and* using visualization. If you integrate both of these strategies into your training, you can reach your highest levels of skill in any area. In this study, visualization was used to improve physical performance. I note, however, that it can also be used in other areas such as strategy development, communication, writing, music, and other endeavors.

Yielding in Work and Career Advancement

To excel in any career, whether you are an artist, an entrepreneur, or a small part of a large organization, you have to develop the necessary skills to help grow the business. There are three areas of importance we will look at here: understanding the strategic vision, setting objectives, and crafting a strategy. The heightened awareness gained from learning yielding skills increases your chance of succeeding in each of these areas.

Strategic Vision

The strategic vision provides an overall picture of "who we are, what we do, and where we are headed." This is the view of the type of company you are working to build and how the business will represent itself. Having a clear picture of this strategic vision leaves no uncertainties of where the company intends to go. No matter what your work or career, having a strategic vision will give you the strength and meaning to overcome the many obstacles that might slow you down.

The strategic vision for my portlandtaichiacademy.com/online-training/ beginning program is "to create a platform where people around the world can learn and be inspired to become more humble, happy, healthy, and live a more harmonious life."

Setting Objectives

You convert your strategic vision into action by setting objectives. These objectives set forth target outcomes and performance milestones. Objectives are important. They are the short-term goals that lead you to the main goals. Without these short-term objectives guiding you in the right direction, you can become discouraged and lose track of where you are going. When I decided to write this book, one of my objectives was to write at least eight thousand words per week until I reached at least seventy thousand words. This was an objective that I could easily follow and hold myself accountable to while staying focused on the bigger vision. Objectives help you in many areas. Here are a few examples of objectives one might use to advance one's career or business:

- Faster revenue growth
- Greater production efficiency
- Increased market share
- Development of a more attractive product line
- Production of a higher-quality product or service

Certainly, there are many other possibilities for objectives tailored to your particular situation, but the list above gives you an idea of the nature of objectives.

Crafting Strategies

Lastly, crafting a strategy is the third concept that helps you create success. We need strategies to help us achieve objectives that will allow us to accomplish our overall mission. Strategy answers the question, "How?" How will you achieve performance goals, outcompete competitors, gain a sustainable competitive advantage, strengthen an enterprise's long-term business position, or realize management's strategic vision for the organization?

When you understand strategic vision, setting objectives, and crafting strategies, you can plan how to move yourself, your work, your career, or your business to the next level. Having this understanding will increase your value, whether you are an employee or an entrepreneur.

How do these three business-related tactics relate to yielding skills? Developing a successful strategic vision would be hard to do without being able to read your clients well. Many times, a person's performance, product, or service outperforms all the others just because of one minor difference. When we can use mental yielding to see behind what people are saying, it can give us insights that we may have otherwise missed. If you are an employee and you bring this enhanced awareness up the chain-of-command, your employer will quickly see how valuable you are. Let's take a look at an example of a minor insight in a business that can stand between you and excellence.

> There was a famous doll maker in China back in the 1600s. Every doll he made sold immediately. All of the other doll makers in China tried to copy his work. However, none of them were ever as successful as he was.
>
> When he was getting ready to retire, he decided to teach his trade to a local young woman in his village. She showed great improvement and listened to everything he taught her.
>
> After three years of training, her dolls were almost perfect. Most people said they looked just like the master's dolls, but for some reason, they did not sell as well, even when others did not know if they were created by the master or the young apprentice.
>
> When the master was on his deathbed, she asked, "Why are my dolls not as popular as yours?" He told her to bring one of her dolls to him and he would show her. When she brought him the doll, he changed the shape of the mouth from a neutral position to a soft smile. From that day forward, her dolls were in high demand, and she could sell as many as she could make.

Yielding helps us notice the details, whether it is another person's expression or in our own interpersonal realizations. When we can see subtleties with a clear eye, it is much easier to guide the outcome toward the positive.

Yielding skills are also useful when setting successful strategic objectives. Oftentimes we are caught up in our heads and find it difficult to practice, learn, or focus. Yielding, by recognizing and moving on from these distractions, will allow you to stay on track to make, adjust, and accomplish specific objectives.

Finally, crafting a strategy is using yielding's situational awareness to take everything into account. How do we make our vision happen? If we are not in tune with our strategic vision, objectives, and possible obstacles, our strategies will be shallow. Our yielding-taught ability to step back and observe the entire game gives us the powerful capability to make the wisest decision.

Achieving Higher Levels of Competition

With competition, you do not learn anything from a challenge in which you do not try your hardest. Growth comes from learning how to deal with and overcome resistance. If you can do this, you reach your fullest potential and will be able to reach for the stars. When competing in any sport at a high level there are sacrifices that you will have to make. You can't eat everything that looks good, go out drinking every weekend, or live life without structure and focus. To be a high-level competitor your physical, mental, and emotional states are always in training.

There are many responsibilities we have in life – work, school, children, financial obligations, and family. These are just a few that we will have to juggle outside of our rigorous training schedule. These responsibilities can lead to self-doubt that affects our physical performance. Yielding is essential to helping you stay positive and keep you on track like a heat-seeking missile. Often times, one distraction leads to another; pretty soon, you have wasted an hour, day, or even more time worrying. If you have the ability to notice these distractions when they first appear and can redirect your focus and energy before they build up too much momentum, you can stay on target, just like a precision missile. Successful competitive ambition is very similar to a child climbing a tree. As a child, you were fearless as you swung from one branch to another, hung upside down, and did the things that make all parents anxious. You felt safe, believing all you had to do was put your hand here or your foot there. You were certain you wouldn't fall so long as you put feet and hands in just the right place.

This lack of fear allows kids to be playful and creative, which in turn helps them to improve their skills at a much faster rate than if they were apprehensive. Even if they take a tumble, they brush it off, get back up, and try again. As we get older, we experience what it is like to face a serious injury and start to focus on the many potentials for error. While a child's physical activities look innocent and fun, for the experienced adult, the same actions can seem to be an injury waiting to happen. Adults think of everything they have to lose if they are injured – lost wages from missed work, a canceled surfing trip next month with your buddies, and other forfeited plans.

In order to reach high levels in competition and push your ability to learn and grow in whatever competitive environment you are in, you have to let your passion and ambition for the activity feed your motivation. If you also use your passion and ambition to keep it playful, you will increase your ability to learn. That too will help you reach the highest levels in your sport.

> *"If you are ready to die, then you are ready to live."*
>
> — RICKSON GRACIE

It is hard to define precisely when a high-level competitor becomes a legend. Yet, for the fans present at the Nippon Budokan Hall on April 20, 1995, that moment was easy to put a finger on. At the end of the Vale Tudo completion in Japan, only one man remained after three fierce battles, Rickson Gracie. He earned a spot in the Jiu-Jitsu record books because of his game plan and established his place while becoming a legend in the hearts of the Japanese spectators.

With that win, Rickson Gracie was acknowledged as the best Mixed Martial Arts contender on the planet. Throughout the martial arts community and for all of those who followed the competition, his win was an emotional event. The Brazilian Jiu-Jitsu master should have won because, up to that point, he had prevailed against every opponent he encountered during the years leading up to the Vale Tudo competition. What made his triumph special, and what resonated with fans everywhere throughout the world, was how Rickson Gracie claimed his ultimate prize.

Yuki Nakai, the smallest man in the Vale Tudo competition, was Gracie's final opponent. Nakai had suffered a serious physical injury to his eye during his first fight with Gerard Gordeau. In spite of being nearly blinded, Japan's most beloved competitor won his two fundamental battles and earned the right to confront the defending champion, Rickson Gracie, in the final fight.

Prior to that battle, Rickson praised the boldness his adversary had shown, calling Nakai "fearless" and saying Nakai "had the core of a lion." Rickson seemed to have a clear path to the championship title. If Gracie simply targeted Nakai's injury with strikes to the head, triumph was certain to follow. This is what many fighters would have done.

But that is not what happened. Instead of striking the injured side of Nakai's face, Rickson Gracie battled for over six minutes without throwing a single strike in that direction. At 6:22 minutes into the first round, Gracie caught the Japanese warrior in a rear-naked choke and Nakai fell prey to Gracie's near-perfect Jiu-Jitsu execution. As their country's martial arts legend lay on the canvas, the audience rose to show their respect for him. They valued the specialized expertise they had just witnessed. However, they roared in appreciation for the respect and samurai soul that had been demonstrated by the champion, Rickson Gracie.

> *"Jiu-Jitsu puts you completely in the moment, where you must have a complete focus on finding a solution to the problem. This trains the mind to build that focus, to increase your awareness, your capacity to solve problems."*
>
> — RICKSON GRACIE

There is an important backstory to Rickson Gracie's legendary triumph of skill and integrity. It was the culmination of yielding's combination of arduous practice and long-term strategic planning. To spread the Gracie message of intention over muscle and strategy over physicality, the Gracie family took their Jiu-Jitsu approach worldwide. To develop the reputation that their Jiu-Jitsu was the best battling style on the planet, they created the long-term strategy of having a Gracie-trained dominant champion in every fighting organization around the world. These champions were trained to not only prevail in battle but also exemplify the discipline, toughness, integrity, and spirit of the Gracie way. In just six battles spread over two sequential Vale Tudo competitions, Rickson delivered the Gracie family's ultimate strategic vision. He was the undisputed ruler of battle sports, a living legend, and the most effective promoter of Gracie Brazilian Jiu-Jitsu.

Yielding skills uniquely manifested themselves in the run-up to the Gracie family's ultimate strategic triumph at the Vale Tudo bout. They practiced a strategic deception worthy of Sun Tzu's *The Art of War*. Prior to the six bouts of the Vale Tudo, Rickson Gracie's skills were kept under wraps. Two years earlier, Rickson sat on the sidelines as his brother Royce, forced three experienced contenders to submit in under five minutes each. This won Royce Gracie the Ultimate Fighting Championship (UFC-1) title.

But Helio Gracie and his family knew that Royce was not the best of the family's competitors – Rickson was. The decision to hold Rickson back was strategic and in line with the Gracie family's strategic vision of having their style of Jiu-Jitsu recognized as the best fighting style in the world. Helio Gracie knew Royce could win the UFC-1 battles. But he believed that had Rickson fought instead, his superior skills would have detracted from the ultimate, worldwide battle represented by the Vale Tudo. His win would have been too strongly anticipated and viewed as a guaranteed, uninteresting, overmatched fight. So, Rickson viewed the UFC-1 championship bout from the corner that night, sitting tight and waiting for his opportunity.

There is a lot more to the Gracie story. However, telling the entirety of their story is not the intention of this book. Rather, the

Gracie family's strategies are a useful way to understand the power of mental yielding. The Gracie's objective was to create resistance all around the world – to get people riled up. They wanted to spark the desire in other fighters and coaches around the world to want to prove them wrong. They used this as a trap.

To achieve this objective, the Gracie family started the Gracie challenge in 1925. This was a strategy to accomplish their strategic vision: that of showing that the art of Brazilian Jiu-Jitsu was superior to all other styles of martial arts when it came to a no-rules fight. Part of the strategy was to typically match a smaller Gracie fighter against a larger and more athletic-looking opponent. Through the years these Gracie fighters defeated martial artists using many different styles, including Boxing, Judo, Karate, and Wrestling.

This stirred up resentment. Opponents became distracted with resentment and aggression, intent on showing the Gracies they were not as great as they were making everyone believe. The Gracie fighters used this to their advantage. In the fights, they yielded to this aggression and defeated most of their opponents strategically rather than by physically overpowering them.

The Gracie's strategy is a beautiful execution of mental yielding skills. They set the trap by encouraging distracting aggressive responses from competitors all over the world. Upon meeting this aggression, the Gracie fighters simply applied their yielding skills to overcome their opponents' attacks. As a consequence of their success, in the last thirty years, Brazilian Jiu-Jitsu has been the fastest-growing martial art on the planet. Back in the early 1990s, there were only two Brazilian Jiu-Jitsu academies in the entire Portland metropolitan area; now there are over a hundred.

Yielding in Soccer

There are many different strategies used in athletic competitions. Let's take a look at soccer and see some of the strategic ways yielding, with its enhanced awareness of self, others, and situations, is used to improve a team's competitive advantage. In this section, we will look at different strategies used in the game.

Possession-Oriented Strategy

Possession-oriented strategy basically means that the team focuses on keeping control of the ball. If your team does not have the ball, they cannot score. Barcelona and Spain often employ this tactic, keeping the ball and not forcing anything, waiting for the right moment to slash the backline. By the time the opposing team creates a turnover, they are so tired from playing defense that it is easy to steal the ball back. This soccer tactic can be exhausting both physically and mentally for the team on defense.

Counterattacking Strategy

With this strategy, the idea is to stay mostly in your own half of the field and suck the team in. Once the ball is turned over to your team, you counter the opposing team by exploiting the space behind them, catching them unaware. It takes a team with speed, discipline, and technical finishing abilities to execute this strategy well.

Defensive Strategy

With defensive strategy, there is an emphasis on defense first and attacking second. Even the offensive players are working with a defensive mindset. Outside backs often do take part in the attacks. One center mid always stays home. The team's strikers are responsible for the initial defense and the rest of the team maintains a disciplined and focused approach to implementing their game strategy.

Offensive Strategy

Offensive strategy is pretty self-explanatory, but let's briefly look at how it is used. Your team is always looking to move forward and create powerful scoring opportunities. Midfielders will join in the attacks, putting constant offensive pressure on the opponent and confronting players, not luring them in.

High-Pressure Strategy

This strategy is commonly used when a team feels their opponent cannot control the ball as well as they can. The goal here is to cause uncertainty and indecision in the other team's ball carrier, forcing him or her to make bad decisions, leading to errors and loss of possession. This strategy is also valuable when trying to shift the momentum and put pressure on the other team to gain the advantage.

Low-Pressure Strategy

With a low-pressure strategy, your team sits back in your half of the field and waits for the right moment to go high pressure. This strategy is a great way to set up the counterattack. Remaining tight and compact as a unit is crucial for success in this situation. This can often lead to frustration or distraction on the part of your opponents, creating opportunities that you can take advantage of.

Exploiting Strategy

Here we want to either focus attacks on the other team's player or position. Maybe you have an attack strategy that focuses on a certain area of the field, or the other team has a player you want to target. Whatever the reason, the idea is to exploit their weakness or create one while feeding into your team's strengths.

All of the above options involve some form of physical or mental yielding that relies on enhanced awareness of your team, the opponent, and the overall situation. Without having the ability to yield in sports, a skilled team or opponent will make you look like an amateur. When a team or athlete can win without butting heads, they are highly respected for their skills. When the USA women's soccer team won the gold medal, they hired Dr. Colleen Hacker to teach the team mental strategies to improve their performance. This was the first time in history that a coach was hired just to improve the players overall mental awareness, the skill that is at the heart of mental yielding.

All of these strategies are important. There is no perfect answer as to which ones are better or more valuable. The goal is to have your athlete or team perform like a chameleon, able to change and adapt to multiple scenarios. This is how they become world-class competitors. This is one additional way the idea of yielding can be valuable in soccer. When you can read the other team's strategy and see how they prefer to play, you can adjust to apply your strengths accordingly. This does not mean move to a game plan that you are not competent in. It means having the ability to redirect the opponent's efforts so that they succumb to your strengths.

Mental Yielding in Eskrima (Stick Fighting)

Eskrima is a martial art from the Philippines with many areas of focus. For purpose of this example, we will focus on the stick fighting branch of the art, which makes extensive use of yielding skills. Stick fighting tactics are the proper applications of techniques with precision to strike, immobilize, and defend yourself against your opponent. On average it takes about three to five years to reach a competent stage in your training. At this point, in no way will you have developed mastery, but you will be skilled enough to perform under pressure and begin to understand the strategies behind the training drills. During this time, you will learn many different drills and work different patterns into your muscle memory. To be efficient and useful, your responses should become instantaneous reflexes rather than requiring you to consider each possibility before reacting. In other words, actions become instinctive rather than consciously decided.

Every action must be carried out as efficiently as possible. In other words, it must be carried out at the proper distance, with the proper timing, and without wasting any motion. To do this, each move must be honed through exercises, actual competition, or with a sparring partner practicing resistance. One can only achieve complete relaxation and fluidity by doing this. A practitioner can learn how to evaluate both their opponent and their own action responses through experience obtained from both training drills and competitive environments.

High-level Eskrima practitioners are competent in tactics. They have strategic responses in place for many different situations and environments. Eskrimadors are trained to execute a series of strategic actions, providing essential information for both defensive survival and offensive finishing ability.

Oftentimes, an eskrimador will begin a sparring match or fight with what is called "reconnaissance" or "exploratory" moves. These moves use yielding's heightened awareness skills to test the opponent for preferred responses related to attacking, stickwork technique, blocking or counterattack reactions, and types of defenses and counters as well as responses to sudden changes in distance or timing. Reconnaissance moves in Eskrima are designed to gather information about the opponent and can include a wide range of strategies such as attacks, false attacks, feints, changes in timing, variations in footwork, attempts at disarms or attacks, blocking exchanges, invitations, and responses to second intention actions. It's important to note that eskrimadors are trained to execute these moves with precision and speed in order to gain an advantage over their opponent.

The term "second intention action" refers to a technique in

which a practitioner intentionally gives the opponent an opportunity to attack, with the aim of countering that attack and gaining the upper hand. This is a strategic move that requires a great deal of skill and timing to execute effectively.

Observing potential opponents during training or competition can provide valuable information on their strengths and weaknesses, preferred techniques, and overall style of fighting. This can help the eskrimador develop a strategic plan for how to approach the opponent in a future encounter. Additionally, by studying their opponents, eskrimadors can also gain insights into their own strengths and weaknesses and adjust their training accordingly. Routine drill responses and actions will manifest in a subsequent fight situation. By watching how others respond to certain drills, actions, feints, and defenses, one can read an opponent's body language (posturing) and determine whether and how they telegraph their intentions prior to attacking or otherwise acting.

High-level eskrimadors use their knowledge of yielding principles to conceal their intentions and mislead their opponents. The most effective reconnaissance occurs during the initial stages of the interaction. This is the time when you respond outside your own customary pattern of response so that you set the opponent up to expect you to perform footwork, reactions, or movements that either will not be used or be implemented in ways other than you initially lead them to expect.

Experienced eskrimadors also make strategic use of their feet. The angle, delivery, and retreat of their attacks are initiated by the feet. The ability to change tempo, direction, and distance, as well as using the opportunities present in the surrounding environment will have a profound impact on the outcome of the interaction. Having this ability to control the situation allows you to direct the interaction and lead your opponent to exactly where you want him to go.

As a deceptive tactic, body evasions with footwork can undoubtedly be highly effective – especially if performed during the very last second of an approaching attack. They work incredibly well as counterstrikes or timed thrusting methods. Although they are often utilized offensively to launch a close-range attack, body evasions and displacements are officially considered defensive actions since they lack right-of-way. A few very common examples are: quarter turn step and strike, duck and counter to the body, and the retreat and entry to counter strike. Eskrimadors learn many variations of these techniques, that allow them to yield to the attack while counterattacking to finish or injure the opponent.

Feints are also very effective stick fighting tactical deceptions. Examples of feints include: fake high and go low, fake high pause and then go high again, or fake with the stick hand and punch with the other hand. Grandmaster Villibrayo was known for having many no-holds-barred weapon-based matches. He was reputed to be a master at setting up the distraction with the weapon and finishing his opponents with his rear hand.

Eskrimadors have used yielding-inspired distractions and other methods for hundreds of years to unbalance their opponents and create openings. Three common Eskrima distractions are: striking with the stick only to open up your free hand, kicking the shin to create a response, or feinting with the left side attack to open the right. I could list hundreds of examples, but I just want you to understand the yielding strategy inherent in the game. In sum, tactically oriented eskrimadors control their opponents by making them respond by attacking or defending at inopportune times. In addition, a quality eskrimador uses as little energy as possible.

Energy management is a critical component in any martial arts or combat sport. One of the ways to gain an advantage is by using tactical movements and techniques to force the opponent to expend more energy than you do. This can include creating openings for counterattacks or forcing the opponent to chase after you, causing them to tire more quickly. A skilled practitioner will also conserve their own energy through efficient movements and technique, allowing them to maintain their performance for longer periods.

One other yielding strategy mentioned earlier and that is worth discussing further is the concept of "Second Intention Actions" used by high-level practitioners. As stated previously, to make the opponent do what you want him or her to do is to control the bout. The second intention is the coordination of both weapon movement and footwork to elicit a specific reaction from the opponent. An example would be to initiate a short attack with no intention of landing the strike. The opponent predictably responds with a parry or (inside sweep) followed by a counter strike to your body. You evade that counter strike as you strike to the head. Actually, the term *second intention* typically refers to a more complex form of strategy in martial arts. It involves feinting or creating a false opening in order to draw a specific reaction from the opponent and then capitalizing on that reaction to execute a subsequent attack. This can involve using multiple feints to create a chain of reactions or intentionally leaving oneself open in order to bait the opponent into making a specific move. The key is to anticipate the opponent's reaction and have a plan in place to exploit it.

All high-level eskrimadors are very skilled at second intention play. It is one of the most important skills that a trained intermediate eskrimador will learn. To become effective in the technique, however, the eskrimador must have a high level of basic skills and an understanding of the applications and techniques of the art. These are the tools that will enable him or her to successfully apply yielding in an effective way. Again, as with many other areas we have addressed, the basics of applying the skills so they are fairly easy to understand, but to reach a respectable level of implementation takes many hours of focused effort.

Although you may not aspire to become an eskrimador, soccer player, or Jiu-Jitsu master, the underlying concepts remain applicable to any endeavor we pursue. The principles of yielding transcend specific disciplines and can be integrated into various aspects of our lives. Exploring these applications will broaden your perspective, unveiling fresh approaches to incorporating yielding principles into your daily experiences. By studying and understanding these principles, you gain valuable insights that can enhance your personal growth, decision-making, and interactions with others. Embracing the universality of yielding empowers you to uncover novel pathways for personal development and the integration of these principles into all aspects of your life.

All of these yielding ideas are just the tip of the iceberg. As you become a high-level competitor, communicator, actor, musician, and similar, you will discover innumerable opportunities for yielding. Most importantly though, is the newfound awareness you will have by implementing practices that will expand your yielding ability. Working with mantra repetition is one of the tools you can use to help discover deeper levels of this awareness.

Mantra Repetition

This is very simple to perform. Sit quietly with your eyes closed while reciting a simple word, or mantra, mentally. If you can do this twice a day, it has been proven to be very energizing. One simple mantra to begin using for immediate centering benefits is OMMM. Try repeating OMMM by taking a deep breath with as much air as you can comfortably, then exhaling with the OMMM sound. Let the sound come from the bottom of the abdomen and resonate throughout the body.

While it is more energetic to make the sound on the louder side, often you may be in a public place where this is not an option. In that circumstance, you can also try performing the sounds subvocally. Everything else about the practice remains the same. Though it will be soft, and the vibrations will be on the lighter side, listen closely, and notice the vibrations throughout the body. When performing this practice, do eighteen to thirty-six breaths. It will only take a few minutes and after one session of focused practice, you will immediately experience the benefits of mantra repetition. You can also use the AHHH and HUNGG sounds. One of the benefits of changing the sounds is to generate different energetic sensations. Another reason to vary the sounds is to gain the various philosophical benefits associated with each sound as I'll describe below. To do this, memorize the meaning of the sound and focus on the mental and emotional inspirations that arise from making the sound while focusing on the meaning.

OMMM

OMMM means the changeless strength and beauty of our true nature. It expresses the truth that we all possess the Buddha's body. From this mantra, we can experience peace, bliss, clarity, firmness, courage, stability, and strength. This sound will resonate in the center of the upper dan tien, which is located in the center of the brain in the pituitary and penial gland. If you are having difficulty focusing on this center, this sound will help you find this area and become more aware of its location. The body is the physical vessel through which we experience the world. It is crucial in meditation because it provides the foundation for stability and relaxation. By adopting a comfortable and upright posture, the body becomes a stable support for the mind, allowing for sustained focus and minimizing distractions. Moreover, bringing awareness to bodily sensations can deepen our mindfulness and enhance our overall presence in the present moment.

AHHH

AHHH means the ceaseless expression and prevailing energy of reality and represents the Buddha's speech. It brings energy, openness, expansion, and empowerment. This sound resonates in the throat and upper chest. Speech refers to both our external communication with others and our internal dialogue with ourselves. In meditation, the quality of our speech becomes significant because it reflects the state of our mind. By cultivating mindful speech, we can observe and regulate our thoughts, words, and expressions, fostering clarity, kindness, and compassion. Mindful speech also extends to our internal dialogue, where we practice nonjudgment and nonreactivity toward our thoughts, allowing us to cultivate a more peaceful and focused mind.

HUNGG

HUNGG means the unmoving perfection of reality's primordial openness. It represents the Buddha's mind and is used for the attainment of enlightenment, infinity, essence, and oneness. The HUNGG sound resonates in the middle dan tien or the diaphragm, located at the bottom of the rib cage. The mind is the centerpiece of meditation. It is the realm where thoughts, emotions, and experiences arise. Through meditation, we seek to cultivate a calm and clear mind, free from distractions and mental afflictions. By observing and understanding the fluctuations of the mind, we can develop greater self-awareness, emotional resilience, and insight. The mind is also the gateway to deepening our concentration, developing mindfulness, and accessing states of profound tranquility and insight.

These sounds can be practiced individually or together. Two ways to practice these sounds together are:

1. Alternating sounds on every exhaled breath. On your first exhaled breath, say OMMM; on your second, AHHH; and on your third, HUNG. Then repeat for as long as you like.
2. With every exhaled breath, you can make all three sounds, as OM-AH-HUNG.

When performing these sounds, let the vibrations resonate throughout the body. This will release tension and help you to become more present. This practice is very grounding and good for increasing your focus. After you are finished practicing any of these sounds, bring your focus to the center of your lower dan tien or lower abdomen and sit in silence for at least three to six breaths. This practice is great to use as one of your daily resets, which we will learn more about when we discuss training strategies, but often it can be used for longer, deeper meditations as well. Having these tools to build a practice that fits in to your lifestyle will help you get the most out of your efforts. Now let's look at how to use the idea of yielding internally to achieve emotional well-being.

4

EMOTIONAL YIELDING

Having the skill set to use emotional yielding can lead to many possibilities. A major component of the yielding approach is self-awareness. Important tools for achieving heightened self-awareness are conscious exploration, meditation practices – both static and moving – healthy sleep, and dream study.

Static or still meditations involve maintaining a physically stationary posture while focusing on the mind and breath. Examples of static meditation practices include:

1. Mindfulness Meditation: This practice involves sitting in a comfortable position and bringing attention to the present moment, observing thoughts, emotions, and sensations without judgment.
2. Breath Awareness Meditation: Sitting, standing, or lying down, you focus on the breath, observing its natural rhythm and sensations, which helps anchor the mind and cultivate a sense of calm and well-being.
3. Body Scan Meditation: This involves systematically directing attention to different parts of the body,

observing physical sensations, and promoting relaxation and body awareness.

Moving meditations, on the other hand, involve incorporating gentle physical movements or activities into the meditation practice. Examples of moving meditations include:

1. Walking Meditation: Walking slowly and mindfully, focusing on the sensations of each step, the movement of the body, and the surrounding environment.
2. Tai Chi: This ancient Chinese martial art involves a series of slow, flowing movements coordinated with deep breathing, promoting relaxation, balance, and mindfulness.
3. Qigong: Qigong combines physical postures and movements with breath control and concentration, promoting flexibility, strength, and a meditative state of mind.

Both static and moving meditations offer unique approaches to cultivating mindfulness, inner calm, and self-awareness, which are all essential in developing higher levels of yielding. The choice between them depends on personal preference, physical abilities, and desired outcomes. In later chapters you will be introduced to different options you can explore when integrating a meditative practice into your life.

As part of yielding, one must be open and physically capable of receiving the awareness these practices can provide. By striving for self-awareness through the mechanisms discussed in this chapter, you can create happiness, overcome anxiety, depression, improve your diet, sleep quality, and make better lifestyle choices. This chapter looks at how you can use the skill of emotional yielding in all of these areas.

How Can Emotional Yielding Bring You Happiness?

This is a very complex question. Emotional yielding, with its emphasis on self-awareness, starts with exerting a conscious effort to discover how you perceive who you are. Oftentimes our perceptions of who we are, are influenced by what others around us are saying. This is the aspect of you that society has given you and the one that frequently has control over your life. Depending on what you think other people think or what you have been taught to believe is real, your mind may be the one telling you that you are unhappy because you are, or are not, something or someone you should, or shouldn't, be.

Often such things cloud our judgment. These erroneous thoughts can spring from anywhere, from religious convictions to cultural expectations, all of which produce a fictitious sensation of sadness. This indicates that you need to ask yourself what will make you happy in order to discover happiness. You must also reflect on the question, "What is making me unhappy in the first place?" For instance, do you enjoy what you do for a living? If not, you may have to first change that.

Oftentimes this change can come from modifying your expectations or how you perceive things. If you find yourself in a position that is just not where or who you want to be, then it is necessary to change the situation. There can never be enough meditation or yielding practice that would remedy underlying unhappiness with your line of work if you don't work to change things.

The first step to becoming a happier human being is to identify and remove the "cause" of your unhappiness. This is where meditation and relaxation help you become more aware and in tune with yourself. It is this newfound awareness that will lead you to an understanding of what may need to be adjusted or changed in your life.

If someone experiences persistent unhappiness, it is often an indication that a deeper transformation must occur. Nevertheless, people resist change – even when it is necessary or will yield satisfactory results. It is said that the average person's thoughts are 85 percent negative – all that valuable energy in one's mind going directly to unhappiness! If we can use yielding to lower this percentage by even 10 to 20 percent, that would be a substantial step toward being a happier person.

Counselors and psychologists are regularly sought for advice. We also frequently discuss all of our issues in great detail. Occasionally, this attention encourages our issues to expand in scope and size. Our discontentment eventually solidifies into a safe haven for us. Your emotional state and how you view the world will alter significantly if you reject this comfort and put happiness first.

This is where yielding comes into play. Its heightened observational awareness becomes your primary tool. When thoughts cause us strife, whether it be in relationships, work, life, or personal choices, yielding helps us acknowledge their negative impact right from the beginning. This awareness empowers you by making it easier to adjust your thoughts or actions in a more positive direction. Without yielding's keen awareness, the thoughts or actions that are causing us to be unhappy will often build up negative momentum. It's what recovering alcoholics have learned – it is easier to stay on the wagon if you suppress the initial impulse to drink the moment it appears. Waiting until after the first drink seldom leads to climbing back on that wagon.

By committing to take this path of awareness through yielding, you realize the right direction much sooner. This is because you are in pursuit of happiness, no longer waiting idly for a positive change to occur without your influence.

The practice of emotional yielding allows you to experience what mystics have called "pure consciousness." It allows you to embrace what brings you joy and peace. Never forget that the conscious mind permits us to wear a variety of masks, preventing our "true self" from identifying the individual concealed behind that mask. The gateway to pleasure is unlocked when all masks are taken off through mindfulness and meditation.

This, however, is a difficult transition. It is the reason that you must be prepared to make dramatic changes. So, does emotional yielding without significant change make you happier? No. Instead, you will find that achieving happiness requires you to build consistent new habits in life. These habits increase the ability to use the skills of yielding. The reward is a state of consciousness that reveals one's true self and true path.

Personal power lies in being aware of your thoughts and having the ability to consciously direct those thoughts. Your mind can be scattered in many different directions. Sometimes you are living in the past, other times you are daydreaming of the future, and once in a while, if you are lucky, you are awake to the present. If you live in the past, those events will affect how your future will unfold. When you live in the present, and you are aware, you will know what you are thinking. Only in the present can you gain control over your thoughts, and it is the present where you can be empowered to channel your thoughts toward happiness.

What can you do to become more aware? There are many techniques that can help us reside more in the present. One simple thing you can do is stop and ask yourself, "How am I feeling in this moment? What am I thinking about?" When you ask yourself these questions, you bring yourself into the present moment. Make every effort to be present in the current moment as frequently as possible. Do this five, ten, or even twenty times every hour. By spending more time in the present moment, you empower yourself to be your authentic self. If you find yourself slipping into negativity, remember to ask these two simple questions.

Another thing I like to do when I notice that I have gone off track is to do a "body scan" to bring me back to the moment. To do this, notice your alignment, tension throughout the body, its movement, posture, and breath. The more you do this, the deeper your physical awareness will become. The more in tune you are with the body, the easier it will become to remain in the moment. I have been teaching for over thirty years and have noticed how everyone has different levels of physical awareness in their bodies. Some people, when you tell them to relax and take a few breaths to settle down, they will try. Thereafter, when asked if they are relaxed, often, they will say "yes." But as I adjust their posture, they realize how much they are unaware of their own bodies. Many times, I will need to lower someone's shoulders as much as two inches because they are jacked up so high from built-up tension that they are completely unaware of.

As you start to experience the secret power of being in the present, you will find that many things start to unfold. Not only does yielding awareness help you see things objectively, but it also helps you gain the ability to respond appropriately with perfect timing. Having perfect timing makes it feel like it was meant to be. We receive answers to our questions all of the time. But, when we remain wrapped up in the past or in anticipating the future, we often miss the answers that are staring us in the face. As you become more aware of everything in the present, you will discover many more opportunities unfolding before you. In this example, you can see how the use of redirection through yielding helps produce a positive outcome:

> Person A: "I think our team should focus more on aggressive attacking strategies. We need to dominate the game and take control right from the start."
>
> Person B: "I understand your perspective, and aggression can be effective in certain situations. However, I believe we should also consider a balanced approach that includes defensive tactics. This way, we can maintain stability and control while being mindful of potential counterattacks."
>
> Person A: "You make a valid point. We shouldn't neglect our defensive responsibilities. Perhaps we can find a middle ground where we prioritize attacking but also maintain a strong defensive structure."
>
> Person B: "Exactly. By blending our offensive strengths with a solid defensive foundation, we can create a well-rounded team that is adaptable to different game scenarios."

In this conversation, Person A initially expresses a strong opinion about aggressive attacking strategies. However, Person B responds by acknowledging the perspective while offering an alternative viewpoint. Rather than engaging in a rigid argument, Person B yields by finding common ground and proposing a balanced approach that incorporates both offensive and defensive considerations. Person A, in turn, recognizes the value in this perspective and agrees to explore a middle ground. By applying the principle of yielding in the conversation, both individuals maintain open-mindedness, respect each other's opinions, and work toward a collaborative solution.

An example of emotional yielding in football can be observed when a receiver is forcefully tackled by a defender, and in response, he gets up with the intention of seeking revenge by delivering a strong hit in the next play. However, instead of acting on his emotions, he cleverly decides to fake going in one direction and quickly changes course, leaving the defender behind. This strategic move benefits both him and his team as he becomes open for a pass, increasing their chances of making a successful play.

How to Change Your Mindset

Meditation practice is an effective technique for tapping into yielding's self-awareness and developing the ability to make changes. Meditation slows your mind down, allowing the tension in both your mind and your body to melt away. This simple act enables your brain to function at higher levels. By slowing down your brain frequency to the alpha and theta states, and then learning how to use your mind at those frequencies, you will be empowered to improve your health, increase your happiness, expand your intuition, and enhance your creativity.

The human brain is composed of approximately 100 billion neurons that constantly fire and rest. There are many different sets of neurons all firing at different frequencies. I previously touched on three brain wave frequencies: beta, alpha, and theta. There is a fourth frequency, called "delta." When you are in deep sleep, your neurons pulse very slowly, in a delta wave of approximately four cycles per second.

Of the four main brain frequencies, meditation exercises deal most with the alpha and theta wave frequencies. Meditation exercises are intended to take your mind from the full awake beta state into either the theta or alpha state. As explained in a prior chapter, the moments just before you fall asleep or, right after you wake up, have your brain functioning in the theta frequency, at approximately four to seven cycles per second. A person in deep mediation can reach the theta state.

In the alpha state, your brain frequency is between seven to fourteen cycles per second. This state is achieved during many active meditations and visualizations. The alpha frequency is associated with imagination, creativity, and intuition. While in this state, you experience many breakthroughs in your meditation journey. In the alpha state, your intelligence is heightened to the extent that you can explore creative solutions to problems and discover new insights. These insights assist in changing limiting beliefs and afford to escape from many of the daily distractions and roadblocks that prevent us from achieving our goals.

Recognizing and Controlling Perceptual Influences

The ability to use your mind to control your perceptions of reality and master your emotions is a skill everyone needs. This is how to make every day productive and fulfilling.

In his book, *The Psychology of Winning*, Dr. Denis Waitley observed, "Weak is the person who lets his or her thoughts control their actions. Strong is the one who guides their actions to control their thoughts." He offers the following as a guide:

"If I feel depressed, I will sing.
    If I feel sad, I will laugh.
    If I feel ill, I will double my labor.

If I feel fear, I will plunge ahead.
If I feel inferior, I will wear new clothes.
If I feel uncertain, I will raise my voice.
If I feel poverty, I will think of wealth to come.
If I feel incompetent, I will remember past successes.
If I feel insignificant, I will remember my goals.
Today I will master my emotions."

When we meditate, we slow down the brain frequencies, so we are able to clear mental distractions and focus on the actions we need to perform to achieve our desired results. During our meditations, we can program positive phrases to increase our mind's ability to function at a higher level. If you train your mind to slow down and heighten your awareness, you can access more of your brain's power, thereby increasing your mental faculties. Positive thoughts bring benefits and advantages that give you complete control over your conscious decision-making process.

Using Yielding to Overcome Anxiety

Exploring mindful self-awareness involves a process of introspection and observation, where one takes notice of their own mental and physical experiences without judgment or reaction. By cultivating this kind of awareness, individuals can gain insight into their patterns of thought and behavior and learn to respond to situations in a more constructive way. This can help reduce stress and promote a sense of calm and inner peace. Your daily routine may be filled with so many tasks that you might find it difficult to allocate any time for self-reflection. However, delving into your thoughts and feelings can be highly beneficial since apprehensions are frequently concealed beneath the surface of your consciousness.

"By going with what's happening rather than expending energy fighting or turning away from it, you create

the opportunity to gain insight into what's driving your concerns."

— BOB STAHL, PHD

By practicing emotional yielding, you cultivate compassionate awareness and acknowledge any feelings of stress or anxiety in your body and mind, allowing them to simply be. By staying with these experiences in a curious and compassionate way, individuals can gain a deeper understanding of their internal experiences and develop greater emotional regulation and resilience. While it may seem intimidating, it's important to recognize that acknowledging and experiencing difficult emotions such as anxiety, frustration, and painful memories can lead to their eventual dissipation. By accepting and embracing what is happening instead of resisting or avoiding it, you conserve energy and create an opportunity to gain insight into the root causes of your concerns. As you gain a deeper understanding of what is driving your anxiety, a sense of freedom and spaciousness naturally emerges. Fundamentally, this entails developing the ability to trust and tolerate uncomfortable emotions instead of attempting to avoid or analyze them. This approach often leads to a remarkable shift in attitude. Repeatedly, your emotions disclose all the information you need to comprehend about them, including their cause, which is important for achieving a sense of well-being.

Meditation is often recommended as a remedy for anxiety, but its effectiveness lies in a way that may differ from your assumptions. There is a common misconception among many individuals that meditation is a miraculous cure-all that can rapidly and effortlessly alleviate their stress and anxiety. The primary objective of meditation is not to alleviate anxiety but rather to develop a state of present moment awareness so you can remain in it. Although reduced anxiety may be a positive outcome, it is only a secondary advantage of the practice. Our anxiety frequently stems from dwelling on the past or projecting into the future. However, during meditation, one intentionally concentrates on the present moment alone.

Quieting an overactive mind is one way in which meditation aids in alleviating anxiety. An individual experiencing anxiety may feel as if their mind is akin to a hamster running on a wheel, constantly in motion but without making any progress. Anxiety arises when we give in to our thoughts and emotions. We often accept them without questioning and become overwhelmed as a result. Meditating helps us shift our focus away from our thoughts and feelings, which may not necessarily warrant the emphasis we give them. Instead, it allows our minds to break free from the cycle of worrying and overthinking, giving us the opportunity to catch our breath and gain a new perspective.

Meditation also cultivates an attitude of nonjudgmental acceptance. The aim is not to achieve a state where your life is devoid of difficulties, as that's unattainable. Instead, meditation helps us cultivate the ability to acknowledge the existence of problems without attaching too much importance to them. So much of our lives are spent reacting to one thing or another. Having the ability to increase your awareness of these unhelpful distractions and still maintain a present state of mind will give you the capability to create the best outcome for yourself.

Using Tai Chi to Reduce Depression

Tai Chi is both a moving meditation and martial art. It is a very effective pathway to yielding's self-awareness goal. Depression is a major health issue in the United States. The 2017 National Survey on Drug Use and Health reported that in the past year, 17.3 million American adults, equivalent to 7.1 percent of the entire adult population in the country, had encountered a significant depressive episode. Of these, 11 million experienced an episode that resulted in severe impairment.

According to a recent study conducted at the Massachusetts General Hospital, the practice of the traditional Chinese martial art of Tai Chi has been shown to alleviate symptoms associated with depression. The study centered on individuals from Boston's Chinese community who preferred Tai Chi over conventional treatments for depression. Tai Chi has a long-standing reputation for its positive effects on stress reduction and anxiety management.

During the twelve-week study, a group of Chinese American participants who responded to advertisements for Tai Chi sessions for stress reduction underwent interviews and assessments to determine their eligibility for the study. The study recruited individuals of Chinese American ethnicity who were fluent in Cantonese or Mandarin and had been diagnosed with major depressive disorder in the mild to moderate range. Additionally, those chosen to participate had not practiced Tai Chi recently and were not receiving any psychiatric treatment.

The study involved dividing the sixty-seven Chinese American participants into three groups. The first group received Tai Chi classes as the intervention, while the second group (active control group) attended educational sessions. The third group (passive control group) was put on a waiting list with no intervention. The suitability of each participant was determined through interviews and assessments. Out of the sixty-seven initial participants, fifty successfully completed the twelve-week study period.

Group one received Tai Chi sessions twice a week. They were also asked to practice at home three times a week. Group two, on the other hand, received twice-weekly sessions throughout the study period, but instead of Tai Chi classes, they attended educational sessions related to mental health, depression, and stress. Group three's mental status was assessed before and after the study period.

After the twelve-week study, the results published in the *Journal of Clinical Psychology* indicated that participants in group one (Tai Chi) exhibited a more noteworthy enhancement in their depression symptoms compared to those in both control groups. At the twenty-four-week mark, all participants were reevaluated, and those belonging to group one (Tai Chi) demonstrated a continued, statistically significant improvement. After the study ended, group two and three participants, who were the active control and passive control subjects, were provided free Tai Chi classes.

How does Tai Chi help with depression? Depression is characterized by enduring feelings of sadness or disinterest in activities. Major depression can lead to various physical and behavioral symptoms, such as changes in sleep patterns, appetite, energy levels, concentration, daily routines, and self-esteem. It may also be associated with suicidal thoughts or tendencies.

As discussed previously, the yielding approach helps break things down, allowing us to stay in the present and maintain focus. It is easy to see how these benefits can help with these symptoms. When we get sad, and we all do, how is it that some people can move on to stay positive and focused while others go on a drinking binge and attempt suicide? There are many life problems that can lead to feeling depressed. We always have a choice when deciding how we are going to deal with these issues, if at all.

If my dog dies tomorrow, I will be sad. If this sadness triggers thoughts of when I lost my grandpa and then to thinking about how I was abused when I was a child, I can begin feeling insecure and unworthy. Trains of thought like this can lead to a serious problem. Such negativity builds momentum when we let one negative thought transition into another and then another. We can halt this downward spiral before it builds up too much negative momentum and creates guilt, sorrow, and regret. We do so by yielding to these thoughts and gently directing them toward a positive outcome. In sum, mediation practice gives you the tools to have more control in these situations.

Sleep and Dream Training from a Yielding Perspective

Deep, restful sleep is a critical foundation for good health and well-being. Meditation techniques can help control your sleep. You can use these techniques daily or only occasionally as needed. These tools can help when traveling in different time zones as well to help you combat jet lag. The use of meditation techniques to help with falling asleep will also help you improve your imagination, which is often neglected in our busy adult lives.

If you wake up in the morning feeling tired or feel a lack of energy throughout the day, there is often a problem with the quality of your sleep. Often, difficulty sleeping stems from poor sleep hygiene, stress, life situations, and the day-to-day anxieties we all face. To consistently achieve deep, restful sleep, most people need to follow the guidelines for good sleep hygiene. To achieve consistent deep and restful sleep you should, if possible, follow these guidelines.

1. Follow a consistent sleep/wake rhythm. Wake up at the same time every day, including weekends, and go to bed at the same time every night. As much as possible, also follow the guidelines for good circadian health, which include following the natural light cycles of day and night and eating and exercising at roughly the same time each day.
2. Do not nap.
3. When you get up in the morning, get out into natural daylight and get your heart rate up.
4. It is important to get some form of cardio exercise every day. Brisk walking, jogging, cycling, martial arts, and swimming are just a few good options. Elevating your heart rate for at least twenty minutes every day has been proven to lower cortisol levels and increase the quality of your sleep. This will also help to rev up your metabolism and increase your energy.
5. To promote better health, consider consuming five to six smaller meals throughout the day instead of three larger meals. Eat more green vegetables, berries, whole grains, legumes, nuts, and seeds. Be sure to eat enough protein. Most importantly, do not go to bed hungry and do not eat your last meal before going to bed. If possible, eat

your highest calorie meals early in the day. Eat something first thing in the morning to signal your body to wake up.
6. Be sure to drink lots of water early in the day.
7. If possible, avoid looking at televisions, computers, or cell phones at night. The light from these screens can easily suppress the melatonin that is released by the onset of darkness. The hormone melatonin is just one of the signals your body uses to know when it is time for sleep.
8. Make sure your sleep environment is cool (65 degrees is ideal), dark, and quiet. Your sleep can be disturbed by even the smallest amount of light.
9. If you still find you have difficulty falling asleep or maintaining your sleep, avoid stimulants of all kinds including coffee, tea, caffeinated sodas, many medications, and dark chocolate.

Any good meditation technique requires mental activity and commitment. Often, when you first begin, you will not see immediate results, so you will need to practice in order to master the technique. When you start using a meditation technique to help with falling asleep, commit to continuing with the technique until you fall asleep, no matter how long it takes. If you make this commitment, it will help offset any natural resistance you may experience. Often there is a learning curve with new things, and it is easy to fall back into old patterns. By making a commitment, your mind will find it easier to surrender to the new practice because you are not giving it the option of simply returning to the old pattern. This step, committing, is very important for your success with these practices.

Before beginning the first meditative sleep technique, it is important to have a clear picture of any possible distractions that may be affecting your sleep. To do this, it is best to acknowledge the distractions, problems, or stressors that are keeping your mind from slowing down and letting you drift off to sleep. First, get a piece of paper and write down all of your worries, concerns, and problems. Next to each of those problems, quickly write down different yielding approaches that could enable you to reach a positive solution. Do not spend too much time thinking about all of the consequences or possibilities. Do not worry about how you would make these solutions a reality. Simply giving yourself something positive to concentrate on can ensure that you are not thinking about problems when trying to fall asleep. Instead, you will be focusing on the solutions. Often, using this practice to program your mind to envision positive outcomes causes your subconscious mind to continue to explore these positive outcomes while you sleep. Thus, you may find that by implementing this practice, you will awaken with a new solution to your problem.

Your breathing can be used to dampen your energetic state. If you can recall ever listening to someone sleep, their natural breathing pattern consists of a longer inhale and a shorter, quicker effortless exhale. The inhale breath is the Yin side of your breath, and the exhale is the Yang side. The inhale breath is a less active, centering, calming, inward energy. As you are lying in bed, relax, and watch your natural breath for a few cycles. Then begin to lengthen the inhale breath and slightly pause for a second at the top of the inhale before releasing the exhale breath. An example of this type of breath would be to inhale for an eight-second count, pause for one second, then exhale for four seconds. You do not have to follow this timeline exactly. It is more important that your breath is relaxed and natural. Every time you exhale, visualize letting go of any tension in your body and then repeat the cycle.

Dreams

A goal of the yielding approach is to increase your level of self-awareness. We spend much of our lives sleeping. With sleep comes dreams, and dreams can be very useful in raising our self-awareness and in finding solutions.

Strange, incredible, even impossible things happen in our dreams. Most people never realize that they are dreaming, nor do they understand the many possibilities that could be explored if they did. If you have ever woken up while still dreaming, you have experienced lucid dreams and, most likely, have seen at least a glimpse of how amazing it can be. Using lucid dreaming in your meditation practice can help you discover many things you often cannot see in your awakened state. It gives you new insights for developing your creativity, awareness, and inspiration. It can also offer solutions to many of the problems you may have. When starting down this path you need to first gather some information and expand your vision so you will have the power to wake up in your dreams more often.

The first step is to begin a dream journal. You will want to keep it by your bedside and every time you wake up from a dream, write down everything you remember. Most people sleep in approximately ninety minutes cycles resulting in about four to five sleep cycles for every six to eight-hour sleep period. As you move through these cycles, you experience dreams. The most vivid dreams you experience are during the REM sleep cycle. Your heart will beat more quickly, your blood pressure will increase, and your breathing will become short and rapid during REM sleep. You may also suffer periodic muscle twitches. You will find it simple to wake up in between these sleep cycles and write down your dreams as you develop the habit of journaling. Then you can go back to sleep and on to the next cycle.

Journaling is important because after about three to four weeks you will start to notice patterns in your dreams. Maybe you will even have a dream that repeats itself. This is valuable information for training yourself to wake up within your dreams. For example, you may repeatedly dream that your daughter is singing you a song. Any number of situations or objects may appear and reappear regularly in your dreams. It is important when journaling to write down everything about your dreams in detail. Include the pictures on the wall, the clouds in the sky, or the words someone speaks to you. Be specific and detailed. After you have about fifty to one hundred dreams logged in your journal, these patterns will be clear, and it will start to become easy to recognize them when they appear.

Starting a nighttime ritual is the next step to improving your sleep quality. The first step is to start mentally programming yourself to be ready to wake up in your dreams. You can glance over your journal and acknowledge all of the common dream patterns you experience. Then say to yourself, "When I see this pattern, I will tell myself I am dreaming and wake up in my dream." Another strategy is to look at your palm before lying in bed and tell yourself, "I am dreaming." Do this a few times every night before you fall asleep. When you are dreaming, you can look at your palm and tell yourself you are dreaming. This will strengthen your ability to control your actions within your dreams. As your control and your ability to have lucid dreams increases, you will experience many eye-opening transformations. A new appreciation for the dream world will develop. Your creative ability and intuition will expand as your awareness expands, helping you to see new possibilities and giving you inspiration.

Having good sleep habits will give us the ability to become more in tune during our waking hours. Using our awareness and yielding skills to lead the mind to our desired state, whether it be falling asleep or being open to what our subconscious is telling us when we are dreaming, will offer many rewards.

Chest Breathing

Chest breathing is a simple exercise you can do anywhere. You can use it as a still meditation or practice it as you are walking or going about your daily activities. First, visualize your lungs. Then take in a full inhale and expand your lungs, focusing on all sides: front, back, left, right, bottom, and top. Let your upper body be relaxed and continue to breathe deeply.

While performing this breath, take in as much air as you can comfortably while staying soft and relaxed. If you are being too aggressive with your breath, you may experience cramping and defeat the goal of becoming calm and relaxed. After practicing this breath for two to four months daily, it will become natural and you will eventually find yourself doing this breath unconsciously, without monitoring. This is your ultimate goal. Once you have reached this point, you can continue with this strategy for as long as you like. There are endless benefits that come with developing this practice. Or you can move to the next breathing practice in this series.

Emotional yielding can be applied in so many situations. The main takeaway here is not to memorize all of these specific examples, but to understand that any internal conflict or decision conundrum can be resolved using the wisdom of emotional yielding. Now that you understand physical, mental, and emotional yielding, the following chapters are going to explore, in more detail, how to use these skills. We will also investigate how to further break them down to see past the surface layer of the idea of yielding. This will help us to understand the underlying motivations behind the many different energies that present us with the opportunity to use yielding.

PART II
LIFESTYLE APPLICATIONS

5

LEARNING TO USE YIELDING SKILLS IN COMMUNICATION

One of the most dangerous weapons we carry in life is a loaded tongue. It can ruin your relationships and career and get you into very difficult situations. Being in martial arts for over thirty-six years, I have had my share of injuries, bumps, and bruises. These things almost always heal. I still remember, plain as day, my fifth-grade football coach telling me, "If you do not do your best and give up now, you will repeat that pattern for the rest of your life." Maybe this was a bit harsh for a nine-year-old, but the point here is that people say things to us that make an indelible mark on our memories. Knowing this, I do my best now to say things that will bring positive energy and growth in other people's lives. In my younger years, I had a shorter fuse, and I did not have the skill set to communicate outside of a thirty-second window. What I hope you learn from this chapter is how to use yielding in your communications, to see the bigger picture, and to achieve the life, job, relationships, and situations that you desire.

Yielding training develops communication skills and teaches how to guide conversations by not taking things personally and by finding the best possible outcomes. Few people can say they do not have to deal with negative people. Some of these people will really work to push your buttons. The question is not whether these situations will appear, but rather, how you will handle them when they do. Will you be able to calmly redirect and lead the conversation? Or will it turn into back-and-forth banter that leaves you feeling depleted after it is over? By learning to yield to insults and criticism effectively, many of the other skills you will learn here will seem to fall in place.

> "To win one hundred victories in one hundred battles is not the highest skill. To subdue the enemy without fighting is the highest skill."
>
> — SUN-TZU

> "Without yielding your friends can become your enemies. With yielding often your enemies will become your friends."
>
> — MASTER SAM TAM

I mentioned earlier how yielding ideas can be used in war, similar to how the ancient samurai warriors viewed their battles. They saw combat as their life's work and as fueling their desire to become more powerful. They experienced warfare as joyful and conflict as a way to build momentum toward achieving greater wisdom and skillful abilities. They were not concerned about winning or losing or even living or dying. They bravely engaged in every encounter, striving to fight with poise and learn from every moment of conflict. By welcoming conflict, they were able to maintain focus, stay relaxed, and perform at incredible skill levels.

While I do not recommend going out and looking for trouble, I do recommend that you study how to be comfortable when it arrives. If someone attacks, criticizes, or insults you, tell yourself it is okay. Laugh it off inside, not allowing it to leave a mark on who you are. If you fight back and resist, you will feed the fire and give credibility to their negative remarks.

We have touched on many ways you can apply yielding in different areas of your life. You may read some of this and think, "Oh, sure, I already do that." I would agree that we do some of these things naturally, but there are vast gray areas where we can learn to use yielding more effectively. When we progress through learning a skill, we transition through four stages of awareness. I want to begin by listing those four stages:

- **Unconscious Incompetence**: At this stage, a person is unaware of how to perform a skill or task, and they may not even realize that they lack the necessary knowledge or ability to do so. As a result, they may not see the importance or usefulness of learning this new skill. It is only after recognizing their own incompetence and the potential benefits of acquiring the skill that they can move on to the next stage of learning. The duration of this phase may vary depending on the individual's motivation and commitment to learning.
- **Conscious Incompetence**: At this level, the individual understands that they do not know the skill and that there is a deficit, as well as the realization that learning the skill will benefit them. At this stage, they can learn from their mistakes, which is a valuable part of the development.
- **Conscious Competence**: When a person knows how to do something, they arrive at this level. However, demonstrating the skill does not come naturally and requires concentration. They need to break the information down into steps and to focus on each specific part of the process to perform the new skills.
- **Unconscious Competence**: This is when the individual has performed so many repetitions of the skill that it seems to be "second nature" and executed with ease.

Often, they will be so comfortable with the skill that they may multitask when performing it. At this level, they may have the expertise needed to teach others depending on how it was learned.

The last stage, unconscious competence, is extremely valuable in fighting. For example, in boxing, you need to practice a thousand times how to respond to someone's jab until you reach a point where you do not have to think about how to respond when it happens in a bout. If you must take even a half-second to think, you've already been hit.

When it comes to communication, however, the use of conscious competence is more important in both your language and nonverbal presence. If you are unaware of your verbal and nonverbal responses, it can send the communication in a direction you do not want it to go. While this may work in your favor at times, sometimes it can backfire. Keeping your awareness in the conscious competence stage gives you more control over your interpretation, delivery, and leadership during any interaction.

A former Tai Chi instructor of mine used to say, "The most powerful love potion is consideration." This leads to the next yielding skill to be mastered: empathy. Empathy is a multi-dimensional and intricate psychological concept that entails the capacity to comprehend and relate to the emotions, thoughts, and viewpoints of others. It involves being able to imagine oneself in another's position and feel what they are experiencing. Empathy involves both cognitive and emotional components, such as the ability to recognize and understand the emotions of others, the ability to respond to those emotions with appropriate behavior, and the ability to experience the same emotions as others in response to a situation. It means paying attention to another human being, asking about their thoughts and feelings, and making an effort to understand their world. This does not mean you have to agree with their thoughts or beliefs. It just means trying to understand the situation from the other person's perspective. Empathy in conversation is the ultimate yielding skill when dealing with another's aggression. Frequently, when someone is tense and displaying frustration, showing empathy will ease this tension.

The ability to listen is an essential component when it comes to being able to show empathy and yield during a conversation. Many times, when we are conversing with someone, we are waiting for an opportunity to interrupt or thinking about what we are going to say next. This is not listening. Being an active listener takes effort and skill. It is important to be open and unbiased, hearing accurately, and objectively interpreting the information before responding. Zen Buddhism offers a story that succinctly summarizes the problem of not listening:

> "It was obvious to the master from the start of the conversation that the professor was not so much interested in learning about Zen as he was in impressing the master with his own opinions and knowledge. As the Zen teacher explained, the learned man would frequently interrupt him with remarks like 'Oh, yes, we have that, too' and so on.
>
> Finally, the Zen teacher stopped talking and began to serve tea to the learned man. He poured the cup full, then kept pouring until the cup overflowed.
>
> 'Enough!' the learned man once more interrupted. 'The cup is overflowing; no more will go in!'
>
> 'Indeed, I see,' answered the Zen teacher. 'Like this cup, you are full of your opinions and speculations. If you do not first empty your cup, how can you taste my cup of tea?'"

When you engage in open and unbiased listening, hearing what is being said verbally and nonverbally, how do you decide the best way to respond? First, many times people do not say exactly what they mean. Mistakes are common if you immediately react to what others say when their words lack clarity or conflict with their body language. This is why it is so important to be able to read their body language, tone, pace, facial expressions, and breathing patterns. If you can read these cues, your response will be more correct, keeping the conversation smooth as you subtly guide the conversation to a positive outcome.

Developing yielding's empathic and listening skills is very important because by noticing these things in others, you learn how to display the appropriate body language and use the right words to make a positive contribution to the conversation. This awareness allows you to adjust how others perceive you. Now, I do not mean to be fake. What I mean is that doing this allows you to learn how to tap into and use your genuine, positive feelings to create a successful interaction. Remember, it's not about how you see yourself acting in a particular conversation, but what others are seeing, picking up on, and responding to in your words and body language.

An example might help to show this point. Say, I am talking to you about a mutual problem and think that I am communicating with clarity and consideration. If you disagree, your response will not be what I expect. You will respond according to how you interpret things, not according to how I do. At this point, I can only deal with this situation according to how you see it. It does not matter if I feel I am right. If I keep trying to show you that you are wrong, and my way is the right way, pretty soon you might want to smack me upside the head. This is why it is so important to actively listen when others are talking, use empathy and be kind in your effort to redirect the conversation.

Research has demonstrated that up to 70 percent of individuals who read a document will misconstrue the precise meaning of the information it conveys. Even more disturbing, eight out of ten people misunderstand most verbal exchanges. It is easy to talk, but often challenging to listen to the heart of the spoken word. Most of the time when you ask someone, "Do you understand what I have just said?" they will claim that they understood everything when, in reality, they are at least partially off track. When you want to ensure someone hears your point, an effective tactic is to ask them to tell you what you have just said. This gives you a more accurate reading of how well you have communicated and how well they have received your information. When communicating, it is your responsibility to ensure that the person with whom you are talking understands what you are saying. If you do not accurately perceive where their understanding lies, it is impossible to successfully guide the conversation in the direction you want it to go. It is crucial that you not sound condescending by implying that you think they misunderstood what you said. It is better to put the blame on yourself. When asking them to repeat what you said, you should imply that it is for your benefit, saying something like: "To be sure I said what I meant to say, would you please paraphrase what I just said?" Most people will gladly do this which helps keep the conversation positive.

Interestingly, a game played in Tai Chi Chuan, called "pushing hands" provides an apt analogy to yielding in conversation. Tai Chi pushing hands has four basic moves: ward off, rollback, press, and push. While simple, pushing hands movements require serious practice to reveal what they are and how and when to use them. During practice, the two participants adhere lightly to each other as they follow the motions back and forth, up and down, left and right.

This communication skill is exactly like playing pushing hands in Tai Chi Chuan. In push hands, we yield to our partner when they push us, redirecting their energy, so it does not put us in a compromising position. This form of listening with the body allows us to notice all of the subtle intentions that are coming from our partner. If we can stay present, it is easy to lead their attack (push) to a position that we can either attack from or immobilize them, so they are no longer a threat. This form of play is extremely subtle at the higher levels and to be good it is essential that you be in tune with every detail going on in your body and theirs.

As stated previously, Tai Chi Chuan is based on the principle of not meeting force with force. Its serious practitioners frequently say one should, "Use four ounces to move one thousand pounds." This principle is based on the idea of using your opponent's strength against them. When someone attacks you with a lot of force, rather than resisting, you use their energy to redirect the attack away from you. The key here is to guide the attack, not to forcefully push it away. This can be compared to leading a bull with a ring through its nose – you don't need a lot of force, just a gentle guidance in the right direction. Similarly, when someone throws a powerful punch at you, you should not resist it with equal force, but instead, you should gently redirect it by moving your body slightly off its course. If you tried to make a major change in the course of the attack, you might get bowled over by the punch's forward momentum. Moreover, even if you were to succeed, a significant amount of energy would be required. By developing yielding's sensitivity to the other in pushing hands, our bodies begin to react and communicate in a way that is similar to how we can successfully communicate during significant conversations.

Upon becoming more in tune with these physical and mental communication skills, we experience how powerful they can be. Most communicators use three points of view to interpret a communication exchange.

- **The Truth:** Here lies the content. It is accorded only about 7 to 10 percent credibility value by the recipient. To you, the truth may be the most important part of your message but often is the least valued.
- **Your Voice:** The recipient's judgment of the conversation depends about 30 to 40 percent on your vocal tone, pace, pitch, modulation, and pauses.
- **Body Language:** The recipient values body language (physical movements, facial expressions, and breathing patterns) the most, according to it about 50 to 60 percent credibility when evaluating your meaning in the conversation.

Certainly, people are more influenced by how you say something than by what you are actually saying. Despite this, it is still important to speak the truth if you want to maintain respect and to have credibility with others. The aforementioned three aspects of interpretation underscore the importance of paying yielding-inspired attention to all three when engaged in a conversation. If we are oblivious to these signals, in ourselves and others, we will misrepresent our true intentions and often misinterpret the message we are receiving.

Once again, yielding's self-awareness becomes a crucial component of successful communication. Given that, in face-to-face encounters, 50 to 80 percent of your communication comes from your body language and vocal expressions, these two aspects are extremely important. Your body language should harmonize with your voice, with your tone, pace, pitch, modulation, and pauses supporting your body language and vice versa. Otherwise, people might view you negatively and not be positively influenced by what you are saying. If you present an average idea brilliantly, it will more often than not be accepted. In contrast, if you present a brilliant idea poorly, you'll find that it is often rejected. Once you learn to break yielding's conversational skills down and use them fluidly, your family life, relationships, work, and self-esteem will all become more in tune with your desires.

It is possible to breakdown some of the body language responses to achieve a heightened sense of awareness in our conversations. Once you begin to notice things you have never noticed before, just observe the information. Do not try to interpret what everything means, because it is not always black and white. As our sensory acuity develops, there are certain physical changes in ourselves and others that will inform us as to what is actually being communicated. These include the following, which will be discussed in greater detail below: minute muscle changes, skin color changes, breathing pattern changes, and lower lip changes.

With most people and ourselves, these responses are fairly easy to see after a small amount of practice. Since these changes are mostly unconscious, they will convey "straight," undisguised information. Of course, many other physiological changes occur besides the four listed here. For example, as we communicate, we shift our weight, tilt our head, move our shoulders up and down, and move our arms and hands; all of these motions are part of our unconscious communication. These more obvious responses are easier to see than the subtle ones. As you start to become more competent and aware, your ability to recognize the more subtle responses will increase. There is more to say about the previously mentioned body language signals.

Tiny Muscle Changes

There is an ongoing balancing act between tension and relaxation, from the small muscles in the face to the larger muscles throughout the body, and even within our internal organs. The shifts in our facial expressions are often some of the easiest to read. These occur at the corners of the eyes (also known as crow's feet), around the mouth (such as smile lines or frown lines), along the jawline, and sometimes around the nose. The deepening of the crease between the eyes or across the forehead is also a good indicator of internal change.

These small muscle changes are not universal to every individual or culture. With consistent practice and by receiving feedback, it is possible to develop the ability to detect subtle facial expressions and connect them with the person's communication and perception. Over time, this skill can be expanded to recognize the level of muscular tension and relaxation present throughout the body.

Skin Color Changes

The use of triangles, squares, and circles in Picasso's and Braque's art may have been a response to the different colors present in the planes of faces. These colors are undoubtedly present and may have influenced the artists' use of geometry in their works. As you begin to observe the slight changes in people's skin color, you will be amazed to discover that they are so apparent and yet, up to this point, so easily overlooked.

Artists study the subtle colors in the complexions of all races of people. Certainly, it may be easy to notice the difference in complexion between a Latinx person and someone of purely Scandinavian ancestry; as our environment becomes more multiracial, we are now learning to recognize the subtle differences in every individual.

By paying attention to such contrasts, you can also notice changes in skin tone and color, which can reveal a person's emotional state. For example, someone who is anxious or embarrassed may have increased blood flow to their cheeks, resulting in a reddish hue. Conversely, someone who is feeling down or unwell may appear paler than usual. It's important to note that there are cultural and individual differences in skin tone and color, so it's important to observe changes relative to a person's baseline rather than making assumptions based on stereotypes or generalizations. As you become aware of the different areas of the face and how the colors vary, you will start to become more aware of the changes within each of these areas. Yielding's observational skills will lead us to discover more subtle changes like flashes of color that will appear and disappear.

Soon, you will be able to detect and understand what internal state or processes is indicated by a particular color change. When practicing these skills use very clear language that will give you a known response. Eventually, you will have the ability to know which changes are positive and which are negative. This is one more way to use heightened awareness that assists in a clearer reading of every interaction.

Breathing Changes

When observing the breath, you will not always be able to see the abdomen or chest movement because different kinds of clothing will make it hard to see. Even in these situations, it is not impossible to use this skill. Shift your attention to the edge of the shoulders and see how they rise and fall. You will begin to see the breath and will be able to follow the rhythm. People breathe differently, some high in the chest, some low in the belly. Their breath comes fast, slow, or medium-paced; can be filled with pauses; and has different rhythms.

If a person's breathing changes during a conversation, it signals that there has been a mental shift. Remember, this too will vary from person to person. One thing is definite – when the breathing shifts in rhythm or body placement, something has changed within the individual.

When you become more in tune with these observations, you will begin to discern the answer to your question before the person replies. The more successful your interpretations, the easier it becomes to fine-tune this skill.

Lower Lip Changes

Look at the lower lip of everyone you interact with. Gather as many patterns, movements, and responses as you can. When you start to see these different signs, you will begin to see patterns, repetitions, and differences in the size, similarities, shape, texture, movement, tremble, color, tumescence, and wetness.

It is next to impossible to consciously control the lower lip. The lower lip sends signals directly from a person's unconscious. Once you have sufficient examples and have correlated them with subsequent responses, you will be in possession of information others will miss. Being relaxed is the key to using these skills.

If you are in a conversation and strain, try to force your face or body language into certain expressions it will not be very effective. Once, a musician went to study meditation with a qigong master:

"The musician asked, 'Should I control my mind, or should I completely let it go?'

The Master answered, 'Since you are a great musician, tell me how you would tune the strings of your instrument.'

The musician said, 'I would make them not too tight and not too loose.'

'Likewise,' said the master, 'In your meditation practice you should not impose anything too forcefully on your mind, nor should you let it wander.'"

Keeping the mind open and present is essential for becoming highly skilled in any form of yielding, including conversational yielding.

Choosing the Right Words

The next step with conversational heightened awareness is developing the ability to use the right words to persuade and to guide the other person's thoughts in a certain direction. Rhetoric refers to the skill of impactful and persuasive speaking or writing, typically utilizing figures of speech and other techniques of composition. Seeing speech as an art form helps us successfully articulate the information we gather from our attention to detail. It allows us to find common ground with whomever we are interacting and articulate clearly what we are trying to say. There are certain ways of being aware that help us deliver our message most persuasively.

The first is your perspective of yourself and your message. How do you feel about your message based on your knowledge, background, experience, and understanding of the subject? Vital to effective persuasion is a deep understanding of your topic. If you have mastered the topic, it is easier to influence people just based on your detailed understanding of the topic.

Moreover, sometimes it is important to demonstrate that mastery initially. When I am teaching a Brazilian Jiu-Jitsu seminar in a room full of attendees who neither know nor trust me, it is essential that I first demonstrate my knowledge of the art. When they see that I have a high level of skill, it becomes much easier to influence them to perform a technique a certain way or to implement a concept, such as yielding, in them. In addition to mastery, having passion and enthusiasm in your delivery is also very important if you are attempting to lead someone in an area that they find unfamiliar.

Also, the key to being able to share your message so that it makes a lasting impression with another is to know to whom you are talking, whether it is a group or an individual. You want to learn everything you can about who they are. This is an approach we use here at our academy all of the time. When someone comes in for their first visit and wants to do Brazilian Jiu-Jitsu, the first step is to discover their motivation. If they want to be a fighter, we talk about how great it is for competition and how you can become a world champion practicing these skills. If instead, they are only looking to do the practice for fitness and maybe as a fun outlet, we might scare them away with that information. Similarly, if someone is looking to learn Tai Chi for the push hands and martial applications, but all we talk about is its meditative benefits, they will likely walk away. In either of these nonresponsive scenarios, the academy will probably lose the opportunity to train a potential student.

Yielding's heightened awareness of the "other" can be very beneficial in business. Imagine that your employer gives you a great opportunity to go introduce a new software your company has developed to a Chinese company. You are extremely motivated to make this relationship work because it means a huge career advancement if the deal goes through. You know the product is a great opportunity for the Chinese company and that the software would save them millions of dollars every year through decreased labor expenses. You are thinking that once you show them how it works and how much they will save, the deal will be a slam dunk.

Not true. If you do not take the time to understand the culture of the organization, you may miss the boat. If you make the effort to understand who you are presenting to, you can guide the presentation so that it resonates with their strategic vision for their company and is in sync with their culture. In this way, you are more likely to achieve success.

Since humans see things from so many different angles, it is imperative that we listen and be present when communicating with others. Sometimes, we can prepare for interactions that we know are on the horizon. In such instances, this preparation is essential. Once the conversation is underway, being able to flow with the moment, like bamboo dancing with the wind, is the ultimate experience in communication. In order for this to happen, we need to use the yielding approach of awareness and being present at a very deep level.

Another skill to build on is the capability to organize our interactions from the introduction, through the heart of the exchange and finish with the conclusion. If we do not have an organizational format in mind, it is easy to get off track. Many times, you can steer things back on course without that forethought, but in those instances, it is much more likely that tangents will occur and prevent you from reaching your intended outcome.

At our academy, every employee understands the desired organizational flow of the initial conversation with a potential student who expresses an interest in one of the fighting arts. First, we offer a warm greeting. From there, we transition into getting to know them. We do this by asking probing questions to find out who they are, where they are coming from, whether they have any limitations or hurdles to overcome, any obstacles they might face in training, and what goals they would like to accomplish.

Once we feel like we have a good understanding of why they want to be a student and their concerns, we give them a brief outline of how the first visit will unfold. Then we take them on a tour of the academy, all the while telling stories and suggesting areas of study that fit their areas of interest. After this, we lead into the first lesson, tailoring the lesson to demonstrate how they can use the practice to reach their desired outcomes. Then, if they remain interested, we schedule them for future classes.

We usually schedule these getting-to-know-you appointments

for one-hour time slots. If we did not plan the format ahead of time, it would be difficult to fit everything in, causing the future student to miss out on valuable information or think our training ability is less than professional.

It should be clear from this chapter's discussion that communication is an art form that benefits immensely from yielding's observational and self-awareness skills. If we can learn to use these skills to make those around us feel more comfortable and to lead them to recognize other possibilities and a more positive direction, our own lives become enriched. By learning to yield within conversations, you will feel better about yourself and those who are close to you will appreciate your considerate ways.

6

YIELDING TO INTUITION – LISTENING WITHIN

There are so many levels of awareness that we will never fully understand. According to brain researchers, the amount of information stored in your unconscious mind is estimated to be more than ten million times greater than that in your conscious mind. This database is the source of hidden, natural genius. To put it differently, a certain aspect of yourself possesses greater intelligence than you realize. It is wise to frequently seek guidance from this intelligent part. The yielding principles and skills inherent in the meditative arts help us to break down the barriers of resistance that hold us back from tapping into this hidden genius.

Too often we spend the majority of our lives learning to look outside ourselves to find the answers to life's questions. Intuition is a type of comprehension that arises in the mind without clear or explicit reasoning, rarely found is someone who is skilled at looking inside and listening to his or her intuition. Yet, intuition is a powerful tool that is useful in many areas of life.

Our intuition is shaped by the unconscious mind, filtering through past experiences and vast knowledge to give the individual hunches; intuition is *not* magic by any means. Intuition is often described as a subconscious process of decision-making, where choices are made without conscious thought or analysis. It has also been defined as a way we think without thinking, making choices that seem to be made in an instant but are not as simple as they appear to be.

The term *gut feeling* is commonly used to describe intuition, which is characterized by feelings that arise rapidly without conscious processing of information. Various scientific studies have demonstrated that the brain can process information without conscious awareness and that this processing can influence our decisions and behavior.

Psychologists believe that our ability to process this information relies on powerful unconscious pattern-matching, where the mind scans the past experiences stored in the long-term memory for similar situations and projects possible outcomes to current events. The intuitive ability to process information automatically manifests itself in many of our daily activities. Have you ever made a long-distance car trip without giving your driving any cognitive attention? This is an example of this phenomena called "highway hypnosis."

I have met many people over the years who have developed their intuition to a high level and have learned to trust their gut feeling to provide inner guidance. Most of them practice some form of meditation as a way to strengthen their intuitive ability.

Conrad Hilton, founder of Hilton Hotels Corporation, is an example of an entrepreneur who successfully used intuition. He made a $165,000 secret bid to purchase the Stevens Corporation during an auction. However, just the next day, the figure $180,000 flashed into his consciousness as he woke up. He quickly revised his offer to $180,000, won the company, and ultimately realized a $2 million profit from the transaction. As it turns out, the second-highest offer came in at $179,800 – only $200 less than Hilton's updated offer. This example demonstrates how intuition may be used to help make wise business decisions.

Great professional athletes are also good at tapping into their intuitive abilities. In boxing, you have to be able to feel the intent of the other person to be good defensively or as a counter puncher. In baseball, you have to be able to anticipate how the ball will drop or curve into the plate. In football, you have to read how the play is unfolding before it actually unfolds. If you talk to any high-level athlete, they will say things like, "I just knew it was going to happen," or "I knew I was going to score." Some of their foresight comes from having performed hundreds of thousands of repetitions and other past experiences. But not all.

Repetitive movement in athletics creates the unthinking muscle memory mentioned in previous chapters. Once that stage is reached, the movements become a form of meditation. Moreover, many professional athletes study Meditation, Tai Chi, and Yoga because they understand the value of the heightened yielding and intuitive awareness gained from these arts. Joe Montana studied Tai Chi to help him focus and, in his time, became one of the best football quarterbacks in the game.

I have had some interesting experiences with intuition. One I will never forget, was when I was training with my first Tai Chi instructor. I was always amazed by his skill – he was like an encyclopedia of martial arts. He studied Tai Chi, Qigong, Eskrima, Jeet Kune Do, Boxing, Muay Thai, and Silat. Upon hearing this most people would assume that by practicing so many martial arts, he would have been incapable of reaching a high level of skill in any one of them.

That assumption would be incorrect. He guided eight of his students to world championships in western boxing and won many other martial arts awards during his career. I always looked forward to our time together because each time he would teach me something new that I valued as if it were gold.

The meditative aspects of studying with my teacher began to impact my access to my intuition in unexpected ways. One day, I was scheduled to meet with him for a private lesson. At this point, I had been studying martial arts with him for about six years. The night before we met, I dreamed we were practicing Tai Chi Chuan push hands using a pattern I had never learned before. I woke up with a very clear memory of the lesson I had experienced in my dream. Trusting that dream-inspired intuition, I repeatedly visualized the dream movements in my mind many times before that day's lesson. Amazingly, upon starting the lesson, my teacher began teaching the exact push hand pattern I'd seen in my dream. This happened about twenty-five years ago, but I still remember it like it was yesterday.

I attribute another interesting story to yielding's heightened intuitive awareness gained through mediation, further emphasizing the importance of listening to your gut feeling.

A woman named Liz was staying at her parent's house while they were out of town. Liz's father had recently redecorated the guest room, with stuffed animals piled high on the guest bed. Liz admired the updates, thinking how cozy it all looked.

Later that night, Liz returned from an evening out with friends and fell asleep on the couch. Around 1:00 a.m. Liz woke up abruptly with a sick feeling in her stomach, and this thought in her head, "Go to the guest room. Get off the couch. You should not be on the couch." She listened to that instruction, got up, and went to the guest room, crawling under all the pillows and stuffed animals.

Around 4:00 a.m., Liz heard some noise coming from the bathroom down the hall. Rather than calling out for her dad, Liz resisted the urge and decided to text instead since her phone was next to her in bed. However, when she received no response, she continued to listen, and heard voices that she didn't recognize.

Despite being aware of the robbery, Liz stayed hidden underneath the stuffed animals for three hours, listening to everything. She even had a close encounter with one of the intruders when they entered the room and turned on the light, but for some reason, they didn't approach her. Liz felt unsure whether it was because she was well-concealed or simply by the grace of God. After the robbers left and began to pack their car, Liz texted a friend to call

911. It's possible that if she hadn't followed her intuition and gone to the guest bedroom, the outcome could have been much worse.

Intuition can often come into play when meeting someone for the first time. Our senses quickly kick in to observe and evaluate information on many different levels, often within a fraction of a second of the encounter. In the first few seconds, our mind may offer a series of deductions about the other person, such as whether they are good or bad, dangerous or safe, someone to avoid, or maybe someone to trust. Research has shown that a high percentage of the time, these instant evaluations are surprisingly accurate.

Intuition is extremely important in law enforcement. Of course, training is needed so that the officers can recognize and counter their own biases and prejudices which can skew intuition in the wrong direction. Once the officers are aware of any possible bias, it becomes a necessity for them to understand and learn to focus on those initial two seconds of an encounter because their intuition can literally make the difference between someone's life and death.

From a law enforcement perspective, it is crucial to be aware of this phenomenon on multiple levels, such as situational awareness, evaluating a witness, and detecting a suspect's deception. Think about all the aspects of communication that arise from body language and vocal expressions that we discussed in the previous chapter, including muscle changes, skin color changes, and breathing and lower lip changes. These conscious and unconscious cues can reveal a person's mood, behavior, and intentions, which can be valuable for law enforcement professionals. It is essential to understand and be able to interpret these nonverbal cues to effectively communicate and interact with others, particularly in high-stress or high-stakes situations.

Because we process observations (via sight, sound, presented, and unpresented information) in our unconscious mind and because gut feelings also come from there, unconscious analysis can happen quickly and leave us confused. We might not be able to reconcile our gut feelings with the conscious messages we receive. Sometimes our intuition might not feel correct, leading us to ignore the intuition. If we struggle to logically justify our intuition, we tend to rely instead on our conscious mind alone.

Regardless of such disregard for our intuition, humans go through life having a high percentage of our decisions made by our subconscious mind. One researcher, Gary Klein, claims that 90 percent of our critical decisions are made using our intuition. He contends that while the conscious mind does contain our subjectivity, morality, judgment, self-awareness, and ability to make logical judgments, it is our unconscious mind that actually controls how we navigate through life and deal with our existence. The unconscious mind is capable of thinking as well as feeling and responding, and this thought process is typically quite reliable. The more rational, intentional thinking, conscious mind finds this cognitive process to be fascinating and perplexing since it moves so quickly.

Sometimes what we refer to as our intuition, gut feeling, or hunch in reality is an instantaneous evaluation of the environment or another person. Often our unconscious quickly notes things that are present or missing, done or not done, evaluating the immediate situation based on subtle cues and past experience. When the situation does not make sense to the unconscious, the alarms go off.

> *"Everyone has an intuition – it's just a matter of developing it."*
>
> — THEODORE ROOSEVELT

So, how does the yielding's self-awareness concept use mediation to develop the intuition Roosevelt believed in? Certainly, intuition is not something possessed by specific people or psychics. Everyone has experienced it. Have you ever been thinking of your old friend Jay only to have the phone ring and it is Jay on the line? Or have you ever woken from a dream sensing that a family member was sick or injured or simply knowing something was wrong with them only to reach out and discover they were, in fact, experiencing trouble? Or, maybe right before you open the cupboard door to grab a glass, you somehow envision it falling and have your hand ready to catch it in midair, without any forethought?

There are many ways to experience intuition just as there are things we can do to improve our ability to be aware of what is being presented. The meditative arts are the most commonly used method of improving this ability.

When I was thirty-two years old, I had been practicing the meditative arts for about twelve years. I had a morning ritual practice that lasted two hours. Maybe I would miss one or two days a year, but otherwise, I was very consistent. It was like brushing my teeth – something I did every morning without fail. Along with this ritual, I incorporated many active meditations throughout the day. I also did yoga four to five days a week and martial arts training every day. At work, I taught martial arts at least four to five hours a day. While teaching is not meditation, moving your body and demonstrating things thousands of times does improve your awareness. Also, studying how others move and learning to break down their movements in ways that can be explained verbally, visually, and through respectful touch enhances your sensitivity as well.

As I dedicated more time to training, practicing, and meditating, I noticed a significant shift within myself. I felt more relaxed, calm, aware, and clear-minded than ever before. There was no longer any pressure to perform or meet external standards; instead, I became deeply connected to my own sense of purpose and direction in life. As I focused on my deepest desires and goals, solutions and ideas came to me effortlessly. As I devoted myself to my Tai Chi practice, I began to experience an increased awareness of my intuition and inner guidance. I found myself connecting with a deep sense of clarity and purpose, with a heightened ability to visualize and take action toward my goals. Regular practice and meditation allowed me to cultivate a state of openness, relaxation, and calm that enabled me to make decisions with confidence and ease. I no longer felt the need to seek external validation, as I was able to trust my own inner knowing and follow my path with conviction. With a deep sense of alignment between my actions and values, I found that solutions to challenges and obstacles presented themselves naturally. I discovered that my mind became filled with distinct ideas and visuals of the actions I needed to take, the individuals I had to communicate with, and the strategies to handle any challenges that might arise.

My creative capacity also seemed to strengthen as ideas flowed into my conscious mind. For example, at that point, I had been playing / writing music for about ten years. At one point I woke from a dream with a song in my head. In line with suggestions in a prior chapter, I wrote down my dreams whenever I woke up. So that day, I grabbed my pen and wrote out the words of the song in about five to ten minutes. There was no deliberation; the lyrics just poured out of me. Then I went downstairs picked up my guitar and started playing the song. I did not have to think of what chords to play or what rhythm to strum – the song was there, fully formed. In less than thirty minutes I had this great song that I still occasionally play twenty years later.

Another intuitive-related experience I had during the same time frame was walking into a restaurant with some friends. After sitting down at our table, I noticed the atmosphere around me seemed to intensify. As I gazed around, it felt as if I knew something personal about every person in the room. The intensity of my perception was like nothing I had ever experienced before. Of course, I do not know whether my perceptions were accurate, but the sensation was so powerful and unique that I have to believe that they were valid. These and other experiences have led me to believe that, by training ourselves to be more sensitive to our intuition, we can come closer to reaching our full intuitive potential.

The regular practice of the meditative arts helps clear out distractions and teaches how to recognize the subtle, intuitive messages from within. This ability to recognize these messages is similar to the ability of a boxer to hear every word his coach says, despite the chaos of yelling fans, the other coach's shouts, and his own need to throw and deflect punches. Similar is the ability of a father to recognize the shout of his lost son over the noise of a crowded amusement park. Our intuition works like this. As you continue to practice these meditative skills and become more spiritually attuned, you develop a greater ability to recognize and discern the sound of your intuitive self. This may come in the form of words, images, feelings, sensations, or other subtle cues that communicate with you at a deep level. With practice, you can learn to distinguish this inner voice from other mental chatter and become more adept at following its guidance and wisdom.

> "The intellect has little to do on the road to discovery. There comes a leap in consciousness, call it intuition or what you will, and the solution comes to you, and you don't know how or why."
>
> — ALBERT EINSTEIN

Our intuition communicates with us in many different ways. You may feel something inside a vision or visual image that comes to you when you are walking down the street, dreaming, or meditating. I often get images right after my morning meditation sessions and after I shower in the evening before bed. Sometimes they are quick flashes and others will last for minutes like watching a movie. Intuition can manifest in various ways, and it's unique to each person. It can come as a sudden thought or idea, a gut feeling, a physical sensation, or even a dream. It can also be a quiet whisper or a loud, clear voice. Sometimes, intuition may not make logical sense or may contradict your rational thinking, but it often holds valuable insights and wisdom. It's important to pay attention to these intuitive messages and learn to trust them. You may also find that you can dialog with the voice to reach a better understanding of the information being offered.

When we receive an intuitive message of potential harm, it can manifest as a chill running down our spine, a feeling of unease, restlessness, a knot in our gut, a tightening of the chest, or even a sour taste in our mouth. Conversely, when we receive a positive message, we may experience goosebumps, a pleasant dizziness, a warm sensation, a sense of acceptance or love, relaxation, relief, or a release of tension.

These physical sensations are important cues that shouldn't be ignored. They provide valuable insights into our subconscious reactions to a situation or person. Our emotions also serve as a channel for intuitive messages. If the information is negative or unsettling, we may feel a sense of uneasiness, concern, or confusion. On the other hand, if the message is positive, we may experience feelings of joy, euphoria, or inner peace.

Being attuned to these physical sensations and emotions can help us navigate life with greater awareness and make more informed decisions. It is important to honor and pay attention to these intuitive signals as they can guide us toward the right path or warn us of potential pitfalls. When your intuition speaks to you, you may experience a sense of clarity or certainty that you haven't felt before. It may feel like the answer is just obvious or that you suddenly understand something that you didn't before. This is because intuition comes from a deeper part of your consciousness that has access to more information than your rational mind. It's like your intuition is tapping into a higher intelligence that can see the bigger picture, and it's sharing that knowledge with you.

Trusting and following your gut feeling can help you make better decisions and choices in life. It's that sense of knowing that can't be explained. Intuitive messages often come with a sense of clarity or certainty that is difficult to explain logically. When you receive an intuitive message, you may just "know" that it is true without being able to explain exactly why or how you know. This sense of clarity and certainty is one of the hallmarks of intuition and is a good indicator that the message is coming from your intuition. Another indicator that you are receiving a valuable intuitive message is when it is accompanied by a feeling of passion or excitement. If you are considering a plan of action but the idea leaves you feeling uneasy, unenthusiastic, drained, or bored, consider those feelings to be a sign that you need to readjust your strategy. Alternatively, if you feel a sense of expansion, energy, and enthusiasm when thinking about the plan, it is a sign that your intuition is urging you to move forward with it.

Intuitive inspirations strike at any time. Particularly valuable intuitive information often arises during the many forms of informal meditation we engage in everyday – such as walking through the park, sitting on the beach watching the waves roll in, watching your puppy run free through the grass, listening to music, or even washing your car. Your intuition is not mystical. Often, I tell students to set an alarm on their phone or watch to go off every sixty to ninety minutes to do active meditations that can take as little as two to three minutes. When you find yourself in need of making a decision, take a moment to pause, take a deep breath, and reflect on the question at hand. Allow your intuition to offer its insight, which can guide you towards the best solution. Pay attention to words, images, emotions, or any sensations that may come to you. Often these images will come to you immediately, but sometimes they may appear later or even the next day when you least expect it.

In addition to inquiring within and regularly accessing your intuition, it is important to maintain a state of mindfulness. Mindfulness is the idea of bringing your complete attention to the present and listen to everything with detail and heightened awareness. It is paying deliberate, nonjudgmental attention to the present moment. Being mindful will allow your intuitive abilities to become more powerful.

The question I often hear is, "How can I possibly meditate with all of the things I have to do during the day?" My answer is to advise the person to schedule a retreat from his or her daily duties to a specific place. In earlier times, such an intention was relatively easy to carry out for many, no matter what their profession. Today, seldom do we experience spontaneous moments of contemplation, and it has become harder to find a quiet, secluded place in which to experience the great benefits of a few moments of quiet meditation. This loss of solitude and contemplative moments is significant since it is the loss of what could be called our natural inheritance and birthright.

It is our natural condition as human beings to need moments of solitude and time to reflect. Unfortunately, many of us no longer remember that experience. We tend to accept as inevitable, the daily grind, the tensions, and the stress that accompanies today's life. We may understand that "to get away from it all" through quiet contemplation might make life easier but too frequently we conclude, for a variety of reasons, that it is not an option. So, we take frantic vacations, dull our thoughts and feelings with substances and television, and do myriad things to distract us while never addressing the root of the problem. These activities are only transitory and of varying durations. They will always come to an end. Many times, upon returning from a vacation, we feel more exhausted than when we left, weighed down by thoughts of the coming Monday morning daily grind.

With this as our present life, making meditation part of our daily life is something that is more than just helpful and instructive. It is something that is practical to accomplish in order to yield a number of important and powerful rewards. Many ancient pearls of wisdom underscore the importance of solitude and contemplation. Meditation is often associated with withdrawal from daily life. Certainly, many traditional meditations were practiced by people isolated from the everyday world, in monasteries or hermitages in the high mountains. Sometimes, their meditative isolation from daily life was only temporary, but still, they experienced it as extremely beneficial. Time away from the social community into meditation provided them with an opportunity to simplify their lives and enabled them to be more helpful to themselves and others.

But what about those of us who are unable to leave work and family while we learn to meditate? Our life cannot be simplified in the same way as can be the life of a sequestered monk. The ability to concentrate, even at the times of the day we set aside for meditation training, is much more elusive for us than for the monk. The situation of the traditional meditation we do is analogous to the situation experienced by a wildflower. Just as the flower is constantly exposed to changing elements, so too is our meditation more vulnerable to the effects of the social environment that surrounds us. Some less hardy strains of flowers and humans do not successfully tolerate these challenges. The ones that do survive, however, will find themselves even stronger than those grown in the greenhouse's protected environment.

Time and patience are very important when instituting the practice of meditation. Without patience, the practitioner will not get very far with the training. It takes a great deal of time to achieve progress in meditation. If you undertake meditation only for the fun of it, you will never reach any depth in your practice. We only progress if we adopt the goals of training ourselves, developing ourselves, and seeking to know ourselves and our own natural state of being. And once we have experienced success with these goals, we must patiently nurture each newfound realization. It is similar to catching a fish. It takes as long as it takes for the fish to bite; so it is with meditation. There is no guarantee the fish will bite on our timetable. Instead, we must simply do the work and embrace the results whenever they come.

By using yielding's self-awareness concepts to develop strong meditative practices you will find it easier to maintain a present state of mind and recognize the positives being offered to you every day. Moreover, cultivating the skill of mindfulness will enable you to maintain focus on those actions that will help you get to where you want to be.

Finally, yielding-inspired meditation helps you enhance your intuition and ability to "listen to your gut." Subsequent chapters will discuss some of the different potential meditative practices that will help you fine-tune your abilities. As you read these chapters, keep the idea of listening to your intuition firmly in mind. Just remember, there is no single right answer or practice. You may discover the need for three or four different practices to help you to develop your skill. So, experiment deeply and listen with a present mind.

7

THE REALITY BEHIND MEDITATIVE INSIGHT

There are many benefits to gain from the practice of meditation. People ask, "Why should I meditate?" There are so many different directions from which to answer that question. I will often tell them if the only benefit of meditation was yielding, that would be reason enough for me to want to meditate. Undoubtedly, there is no one answer to this question that will satisfy everyone.

Arizona's Superstition Mountains are a tricky place to hike. This is because their peaks and ridges are so sharp, they cannot serve as landmarks. A minor shift in the sun's angle or a side step by a hiker completely changes the landscape. So, it is with meditation, every individual will see and approach it differently because they are coming at it from their own unique perspective.

I often explain meditation in terms of education. There are many different levels and directions you can take your meditation practice to accomplish myriad different outcomes. Traditional education offers an advancement track that goes from high school to undergraduate college, to graduate school for a master's or doctorate, followed by postgraduate specialization in the field. The same opportunities for advancement occur in meditation practices.

Likewise, the educational system recognizes that there are many different needs in the community, so it offers a variety of education platforms that provide foundations for students who want to follow many different paths in life – academic, social, vocational, recreational, or specialized in nature. The meditation field is also very broad in its offerings, encompassing many different purposes.

Likewise, meditation practices also serve a broad range of purposes. Many times, when I speak with people about meditation and their vision of what meditation is about it can be very simplistic, kind of like saying everything you learn in education you can get by the third grade. For example, meditation can be used as a relaxation exercise to help overcome anxiety, depression, and other stress-related disorders. Meditation can also be combined with breathing exercises that can be used for physical and psychological therapy. Meditative arts, like Qigong, have been used for hundreds of years to help with insomnia, high blood pressure, influenza, asthma, and many other ailments. However, meditation is not just a how-to-cure-yourself kind of activity. It also improves your ability to concentrate, which can enhance every aspect of your life.

I often will hear people argue that, because they are already at peace, they have no need to incorporate meditation into their lives. They ask, "Why should I make my life more complex by starting something that takes so much time and effort to learn when I am fine just as I am?" This is similar to those who say they do not need further education because they are content with what they already know.

Certainly, a person may find comfort in their ignorance because it does not challenge them to grow nor threaten their certitude. But does anyone who chooses not to live up to his or her potential truly enjoy his or her life? Perhaps such willful ignorance has trapped a potentially gifted musician, someone whose deepest desire lies in gifting melodies to humanity. If that potential musician refuses to learn how to play or read music or understand how musical patterns are created, he or she may never experience their most deeply desired life. A willingness to step into the unknown, to learn something new, presents an opportunity to discover that hidden desire and potentially blossom into an amazing musician.

The same is true with meditation. Its benefits can only be discovered and experienced by those who take the plunge and put in the time and effort. Advanced meditation practices are analogous to graduate school where the student focuses on particular areas of study and ways of thinking. In each meditation arena, we master the techniques and methods while recognizing there is still more to learn. Through advanced meditation techniques, we learn to explore different philosophical applications after having increased our self-awareness of both our bodies and our minds. This allows us to examine our lives through a lens that few will ever acquire. Our devotion to the practice, along with our natural ability, will lead us to many discoveries no matter what meditation method we choose to follow.

Albert Einstein once said: "If my theory of relativity proves correct, my associates will call me a genius, Americans will call me a friend, and Germans will call me a German. If my theory proves false, my associates will call me a fool, Americans will call me a German, and Germans will call me a Jew."

This statement reveals that Einstein had chanced investing his life and future in an endeavor where, if he succeeded, he would greatly benefit the human race, receive recognition, and find physics' equivalent to enlightenment. He also knew that failure would yield recrimination and ridicule. Einstein's greatness was not only attributed to his life's work but also to his daring pursuit of enlightenment, serving as a reminder that although reaching enlightenment through meditation may be unlikely, the pursuit of such a lofty goal is worth the effort. Along the way, our efforts will yield a number of benefits.

Although traditional education has been presented as an analogy to explain certain ideas of meditation, and to describe meditation in general, this analogy offers only a partial view. Education advances through an accumulation of knowledge and by building on past understandings. A person who wants to play the violin first must learn how to hold the instrument, then how to read music and play a tune. In time, the budding musician is able to express feelings through the music. However, this is only the beginning. Improvement and learning will continue for the musician's lifetime.

Sir Isaac Newton, near the end of his life, after major contributions to the study of mathematics and physics, said he had "merely found one shell on the vast seashore." Similarly, Zhuang Zhou, a famous Chinese philosopher, said: "Life has a limit, but knowledge is without limit. When mortals pursue the unlimited, they must not expect to be able to ever comprehend it completely."

Not only are our lives here on earth limited, but our senses, the means by which we understand the world, are also limited and easily distracted. Although we may try to focus on a story, a piece of music, or what someone else is saying, our understanding remains incomplete. Our ears will hear the distant sounds, our eyes will follow the passing plane and our minds will wander, thinking about the past or projecting into the future. Our consciousness is a weak fist and cannot hold the immense amount of information we encounter during our limited lifetime.

Traditional education is always limited, even when the student relentlessly strives to accumulate more and more knowledge. Through consistent effort, meditation offers a different approach to acquiring helpful knowledge. Unlike knowledge gained by traveling the traditional educational path, the knowledge gained through meditation is of different quality and nature. Words are inadequate to fully encompass the knowledge that comes from a deeply meditative experience. Words alone are insufficient to describe it. Conscious knowing is insufficient. Simply put, meditation is a pathway into a world that exists beyond the power of words to describe it and beyond the human ability to consciously acquire information about it. To discover and experience that world is what Buddha called "enlightenment."

To reach an enlightened state of being requires letting go of our perceptions of reality and opening up to the possibility that there is another dimension of reality that we can tap into. The following is a lengthy but instructive story told by one of my Qigong teachers. It concerns a young man seeking instruction from a master of archery. I like this story because no matter how much we learn, without experience and time, our knowledge will never reach the level of the master.

> There was a young man named Shen Lu from a village in the Wudang mountains, who wanted to learn archery. There were stories of a famous archery master who lived in northern China, and he decided to go find the master to ask him to teach him. Shen Lu left his family in the Wudang mountains to search for this famous master in northern China.
>
> After months of searching, Shen Lu found out where the master lived. When he arrived at his house the old master was sitting at the edge of a pond. When Shen Lu approached the master he asked, "What can I do for you, young man?"
>
> Shen Lu kneeled down and said, "I am Shen Lu. I have searched for months to find you to ask if you will accept me as a student and teach me archery."
>
> The master replied. "That will not be possible. I am old and do not have the skills I once had. You should go home."
>
> Shen Lu did not get discouraged easily. "Master," he said, "I humbly beg you to reconsider. I will be loyal and will follow your guidance. I have left my family to care for our farm. I cannot return until you accept me as your student."
>
> The master walked back to his house, leaving Shen Lu kneeling by the pond. Shen Lu was determined and remained kneeling waiting for the master's return. Before long it was dark, and it began to snow. Shen Lu was tired and hungry, but he did not move. One day passed and then another and finally the old master returned. He said: "Shen Lu, if you truly want to be my student, you must first complete three tasks."
>
> Shen Lu was extremely happy, believing his destiny was starting to blossom.

"Of course, Master," said Shen Lu. "What would you like me to do first?"

"Your first task is easy. Simply go home and every night and every morning watch three incense burn. Do this every day and in three years come back to see me."

Shen Lu returned to his family and did as the master asked. In the beginning, it was very difficult; he had to force himself to be patient and wait for the incense to burn out. Shen Lu was determined so he stayed on task watching every night and every morning. Months passed and watching the incense became a habit and he started to enjoy it. He began to understand that when he enjoyed it, his concentration was improving. All of the external distractions began to disappear, and the incense seemed to get larger and larger. He started noticing things that he was never aware of before, like how the smoke spiraled away from the stick and subtle smell of the smoke as it filled the air.

This taught him a very important lesson that every good archer must know: how to be present and calm down the mind, not letting distractions interfere with his focus.

Three years passed, and Shen Lu went back to northern China to see the master. He was excited to let the master know he had successfully finished his first task. When he arrived, the master came out to greet him.

"Did you finish your task?" asked the master.

"Yes, master, and I understand why focusing on the incense is so important."

"And what did you learn from watching the incense?" said the master.

"My focus improved, and I was able to see things I had never noticed before."

"Nice!" replied the master. "Your second task will be to go home and watch your wife weave her loom. Follow the shuttle as it moves back and forth with your eyes. After three years, come back to see me again."

Shen Lu returned to home and did as the master asked. It was very difficult in the beginning. The shuttle moved very fast, and it was hard for him to follow. His eyes would ache when he tried to keep up with the movement. After a year had passed, it began to appear as if the shuttle were moving slower and became easier to follow.

Without realizing it, Shen Lu had learned another valuable skill that every good archer needs to know: how to focus on a moving object.

Another three years had passed, and Shen Lu went back to visit his master. The old master asked, "What did you learn from the second task?"

"At first, the shuttle was very difficult to follow. I had a hard time keeping my eyes focused," said Shen Lu. "As time went by, it became slower and it seemed as if it was barely moving at all."

"Excellent!" replied the master. "Your final task will be to go home and make ten rattan rice baskets every day. After three years, come back to see me."

Chinese rice baskets are extremely difficult to make. It requires very strong arms, wrists, and grip strength. It is a difficult task for most people to make five baskets in one day, and Shen Lu had to make ten.

In the beginning, Shen Lu did not get much sleep because it would take him all day and half the night to complete ten baskets. He had blisters on his hands and his arms were always sore. After six months, his strength improved, and by the end of the first year, he was easily making ten baskets a day. By the end of the third year, he was so strong he could make twenty baskets per day.

Shen Lu went back to visit his master in the north. The master asked, "You have done well and completed all of the tasks. There is nothing further I can teach you." Then the master turned and walked away.

Shen Lu suddenly realized that the three tasks that he completed were his training. He had learned to quiet his mind, track a moving target, and developed a strong body so he was steady when drawing a bow.

Shen Lu was not convinced that the master had taught him everything he could, so he decided to test the master. The old master was about one hundred yards away, so Shen Lu pulled out an arrow and shot it at the master's hat.

The master could hear the arrow cutting through the air. Quickly, he drew his bow and shot Shen Lu's arrow out of the air and watched it fall to the ground. Shen Lu tried again and like the first arrow the master shot it out of the air.

Shen Lu saw that the master did not have any more arrows so he tried one more time and thought for sure he would strike the master's hat. The master calmly broke a branch off a nearby tree and using it like an arrow again, shot down Shen Lu's arrow a final time. Shen Lu ran to the master and knelt before him and said, "Master, I have learned one more important lesson from you. One thing I cannot learn from you is your experience."

The master replied, "Yes, that I cannot teach you. You can only gain experience through your practice."

After many more years of practice, Shen Lu became one of the greatest archers in Chinese history.

I like this story for three reasons. First, it teaches us that we need to put in the effort to grow from our experience. Second, it demonstrates that, if we look closely, we can find hidden treasures in many areas of our life. Shen Lu would have never thought to watch his wife weaving, but doing so taught him a valuable lesson. Finally, the other idea to pull from this story is how important it is to be consistent and work at the simple things until they are mastered. This last point is where the story's true gold lies. How many people can handle the boredom of watching burning incense for three years or whatever it is they need to do to get good at something? If they can't do one thing repeatedly until they get good at it, how do they ever expect to experience the happiness that comes with achieving excellence in a difficult skill?

In Chinese philosophy, enlightenment is reached only after the seeker is able to let go of prior attachments and ways of perceiving things. This emotional discarding of what has been gained in order to receive something new is a fundamental process in Chinese philosophy. This process of letting go followed by an "ah-hah" realization is something that repeats itself over and over in meditation. As each new awareness or higher consciousness is achieved, a new level of perception is created. But it is transitory. You remain at this stage of awareness until you are able to release your attachment to where you have arrived. Once you do that, you are able to move on to an even higher level of awareness. Every time your awareness undergoes this evolutionary advancement, your previous level of understanding will seem trivial and unimportant.

There are many meditation techniques that have been developed to help us experience increased self-knowledge through discarding prior attachments. Traveling the meditation path is similar to learning Jiu-Jitsu. In that martial art, in order to develop dexterity throughout, the body must become coordinated on both the right and the left sides. In Jiu-Jitsu, when you learn a new technique, one side is always quicker to learn a movement than is the other side. If the technique is essential for development in the art, the focus is turned on doing more repetitions on our weak side. This develops equalized efficiency in the movement and more balanced attacks and defenses. This equalizing training creates better balance and coordination throughout the body.

Jiu-Jitsu relies on muscles, speed, and timing to be successful. Like meditation, it progresses through steps. In order to move the torso, the practitioner first learns to move his or her hands and feet by expressing intention within the torso. The extremities move only as the torso expresses the essence of the movement to them. Here the techniques are used to develop physical coordination and agility in the body. Eventually, the more subtle internal energy known as Qi comes into play. In order to develop a higher level of mental skill with Jiu-Jitsu, the self-awareness must shift from the outside manifestations to the inside. Neither the extremities nor the body act independently; both follow the intention led by the mind. Thus, the student's awareness transitions through various stages, imprinting the muscle memory, then forgetting so as to shift to the next stage, moving the emphasis from the hands to the torso, to the whole body, and finally, to the mind.

We have looked at how meditation, unlike traditional forms of education, does not involve accumulating more knowledge. But rather involves "letting go" of information previously acquired. This awareness of how meditation evolves comes from the understanding that every person is born with a special "mental space," an area in the mind suited to peaceful contemplation. As we get busy in our day-to-day lives, this space gets filled with a great deal of unnecessary information, such as thoughts about how we will meet our financial obligations, how we will help our children through a difficult stage in life, or anxieties about the future. These thoughts and memories accumulate throughout the years as a byproduct of living.

Having our minds filled with all of these life situations and matters concerning our existence tends to make us put great importance on these things and often leads to us being rigid in our ways. You could also say that we tend to hold on to the ideas being stored in our mind, causing us to resist new ideas that fall outside of our comfort zone. Consider the stereotype of a senior citizen – someone set in his ways and conservative by nature. By analogy, the older one becomes, the more crowded and filled his or her mind becomes, meaning there is little room left for anything new.

Meditation techniques are used to clear our cluttered minds and allow the mind to experience peaceful contemplation. In Qigong terms, meditation helps us return to Wuji or the void. Once we achieve a void state of existence, there is room for us to adopt a new approach to thinking, one that allows us to dwell in what the Taoists call the "Yin state of mind." Yin energy is characterized as being soft, slow, reflective, receptive, and compassionate. It is nurturing, receptive, and allowing, creating a space for things to be held and received.

This process of cleaning the mind is like cleaning out your house that has gotten cluttered with possessions after years of acquisition. It is common for most of us to accumulate possessions. After several years of haphazardly purchasing one thing after another, we have so much stuff lying around it is hard to just relax and enjoy the space we have available. Think about the last time you thoroughly cleaned the house, unloading everything you did not need. Remember how difficult it was to throw some things away? Even that old disco shirt you have not worn in eighteen years but thought that someday you might want to wear it again? Consider another time when you let go unnecessary, unused items and clutter. In contrast, how did you feel then?

The task of cleaning out the unneeded thoughts in your mind is of a different and much more difficult nature. Clearly, it is easier to give that old disco shirt to Goodwill than it is to stop being preoccupied with the death of a loved one. We also tend to hold on to certain beliefs, behaviors, and attitudes for a myriad of psychological reasons. The following story helps explain this idea.

> There was a well-respected man in the community who seemed to have all of his material desires satisfied.
>
> He had a beautiful home, a loving family, and many servants. However, he felt dissatisfied, so he decided to pursue enlightenment.
>
> First, he decided to give away all of his material possessions and accumulated wealth. He believed that in order to attain enlightenment, he had to let go of these distractions. Finally, he decided to abandon his family and leave the comforts of everything he knew. Leaving with only a small bag with a few possessions, he searched the countryside for teachers and wisdom that would help him attain peace and enlightenment.
>
> For nearly twenty years, he traveled the countryside, searching for wisdom that would help him reach enlightenment. He studied texts, followed a variety of teachers, and adopted many meditative practices.
>
> One day, he saw a beautiful, clear pond and thought how

refreshing it would be to take a swim. He took off his clothes and set his bag near a tree by the pond.

As he laid his bag down, he felt different. It gave him a sense of relief and ease. He realized why he had been searching for twenty years without ever discovering enlightenment.

He thought to himself. "I gave up my family, house, possessions, and wealth, yet, for twenty years I could not let go of this bag." Immediately, he attained the enlightenment that he had spent the last twenty years searching for. The bag symbolizes that which one cannot let go of; it was his final attachment.

It is this bag that represents a person's final attachment, the accumulation of worldly knowledge. It is only when we can give up everything, including ourselves, that we can be free of the attachments that clutter our mental space and keep us from realizing spiritual freedom. We must learn to recognize these subtle pulls of distraction, so we know what to release and what to guide in a positive direction. It is through the meditative arts that we can develop this awareness that will give us the fundamental tools needed to use the concept of yielding to let go of these distractions.

As we begin to open our minds to things that are not part of our daily norm, it is amazing how we start to see things from a different perspective. This is a story one of my Qigong teachers used to tell us. Notice how it attempts to portray time by using spatial and temporal references or by referencing the ongoing patterns within the natural world:

> This story begins on a warm spring morning in a beautiful valley by a still green pond. Under the shade of a weeping willow, hundreds of tadpoles are swimming in the water. An adult spotted frog jumps in the water, joining her tadpoles from the muddy bank. All of the tadpoles gather around their mother asking many questions. "What have you experienced in the world above the water?" "Please tell us what is was like!" They all eagerly await as she begins to speak.

"It is beginning to get warm in the world above. There is a huge ball of fire in the middle of an endless bright blue sky called the sun. It is so refreshing to sit in the mud on the edge of the pond a feel the warmth of the sunshine down on my back. There is a slight breeze that stirs up the water and occasionally you can see fish jump out of the pond hoping to catch a bug hovering over the water. Around the pond you can see flowers, trees, fields of grass, and mountains off in the distance. You can smell the sweet fragrance of the flowers as the breeze blows over your back. You can hear the wind blowing through the trees, the sound of buzzing bees and dragonfly wings as they fly through the air. Yes, my children, it is a big, beautiful world, full of mysteries and endless amazing discoveries."

"What is the bright blue sky?" Asks the tadpoles. "What are the trees?" "What is a bug?" "What is the smell?" "How do you hear the wings of dragonfly's or feel the wind?"

They all had so many questions waiting with excitement to learn about the world above the water. Their mother began to get irritated telling them, "I will not answer any more questions; you are too young to understand. The day will come when you drop your tails and maybe you will see for yourselves."

It did not take long before one of the tadpoles outgrew his tail and went out of the water to explore. The young tadpole rested at the edge of the pond feeling the warmth of the sun, smelling the flowers, and listening to the buzzing of the bees. The young frog took in all of the new sensations and enjoyed every moment. He did not have to be told how.

Those who successfully experience a deep, meditative state find that, when in a meditative state, their experience of time is markedly different. As ordinary people understand time, it is linear – one minute follows the other, with no deviation. As we try to wrap our minds around the concept of nonlinear time, our understanding is hampered by the fact we exist in a three-dimensional world: height, depth, and width. We are left with a sense of curiosity, like a school of tadpoles pondering about a world beyond their own. Unless we discover how to "drop our tails" and begin to experience something beyond three-dimensions, nonlinear time will remain a subject of speculation for us. It will remain as inconceivable to us as the world above the water appears to the water-bound tadpole.

Where and how far can meditation take humans? We don't know the answer. Cosmologist Carl Sagan theorized that there is a fourth physical dimension that we cannot access because we are only three-dimensional beings. We have all heard of the amazing physical feats of yogis. A yogi is a practitioner of meditation originating in the Hindu, Buddhist, and Jain religions. Some have been known to stop their hearts, their breathing, or to physically change the size of their arteries. Some claim to travel through time and space, and to prove it, they have provided the information they could not have known otherwise. Most claim meditation transports them to another plane of existence, to what Carl Sagan might call the "fourth dimension." There are many such stories of yogi feats, but they are too numerous to detail here.

Certainly, recent science has identified physical manifestations of inexplicable mysteries. For example, imagine two paired photons – one positively charged, one negatively charged. Scientists separated them and moved them some distance apart. When the scientists reversed the charge in one photon, they were amazed to discover that its mate simultaneously reversed its charge so as to maintain the positive-negative balance between them. Another inexplicable phenomenon occurs when photons are shot at a wall with holes in it. On the other side of the wall is a plate that registers where the photon has gone through a hole and hit the plate. If no one is watching the experiment, the photon travels a different path than when it moves under observation. Can we rationally explain the feats of the meditating yogis or the behavior of photons? No. I tell you about these situations to underscore the fact that much that is mysterious in the universe can be experienced. And, that some of these mysteries have been experienced by people who have used mediation to reach phenomenally deep levels of awareness.

I bring up this point not to encourage you to spend your life hoping to reside in a four-dimensional world of enlightenment. Instead, I hope to encourage you to let go of the idea that reality is only what you have come to think it is – because each individual has a different perspective on that same reality and because it appears that both mystics and scientists have discovered many inexplicable mysteries in life. That being the case, it is important that we learn to let go of our certitude and begin to be still and listen, so we come to see and experience reality from multiple perspectives.

8

TAI CHI CHUAN AND QIGONG THEORY

Inevitably a student, one who has experienced positive physical, mental, and spiritual changes as a result of yielding training, will ask why the changes are occurring. As stated previously, the yielding concept is an essential tenet of Chinese philosophy and martial arts. This chapter is a brief overview of the basics of the energetic forces and philosophical ideas that underlay the yielding concept. Having a conceptual understanding of these basics will enable you to reach deeper levels of training no matter which practices – Tai Chi, Qigong, meditation, or other practice – you adopt as a way to acquire yielding skills.

This chapter begins by introducing certain necessary definitions, then moves on to theory and finally ends with an overview of applications. The first such progression references Tai Chi Chuan principles. The second such progression relates to philosophical aspects particular to Qigong. The latter, Qigong, incorporates all of Tai Chi Chuan's underlying principles and adds a few more. Please bear in mind that this is a general overview. As you progress in your training you will want to delve deeper into the concepts set forth below. Some worthwhile texts to pursue are listed in the bibliography that appears at the end of this book.

Defining the Overarching Principles

Wuji

As stated previously, most people are familiar with the Yin and Yang symbol. What is less known is the concept of Wuji. Wuji refers to a state of emptiness or can be represented by any singular point in space. Within the human body, Wuji is believed to reside in the center of the intestines about three inches below the navel, the same place as the body's center of gravity, often referred to as the lower dan tien.

There is no polarity within Wuji – it is immutable and singular. Many Eastern philosophers believe that originally, the universe was in an unchanging Wuji state. You are not mistaken if you discern a similarity between this ancient Eastern concept and astrophysics' "Big Bang" origination theory of the universe.

Yin and Yang Symbol

Yin-Yang symbolizes the forces of nature and is the foundation of Tai Chi Chuan. The Yin and Yang symbol depicts two complementary natures – simultaneously opposing and connected. The symbol's curving line is a manifestation of the fact that they are not absolute or non-changing like Wuji. Instead, they are ever-changing and dynamic. The small circles or "seeds" containing each side's opposite hue and appearing in the leading curve of each, signifies that Yin can become Yang and Yang can change into Yin. Regardless of this ever-changing dynamism, Yin and Yang create a single wholeness and cannot exist apart from each other. They are also unceasingly dynamic. In martial arts, if there is no Yin and Yang exchange, your energy will be stagnant, leading to easy defeat at the hands of your opponent.

Moreover, whether something is Yin or Yang depends on the observer's perspective and interpretation. You have the ability to adjust or modify your own perspective of what is Yin or Yang. Finally, whenever the dynamism of Yin and Yang mixes with the stillness of Wuji, changes begin to occur.

Yin Principle

Yin energy is characterized as yielding, cool, and sustaining and is enhanced by inhaling. In martial arts, it is considered "insubstantial." It is associated with water and is considered a purer energy. It promotes a steady, calm, and wise state of mind by lowering the body's Yang energy. However, an excess of Yin energy, one that overpowers and quenches all Yang energy, results in death.

Yang Principle

Yang energy is characterized as active, hot, and creative. Yang is enhanced by exhaling. In martial arts, it is considered "substantial."

Xin Mind

The word *Xin* refers to the physical heart, but within ancient Chinese philosophy, the heart was considered the center of human cognition. Today, in Chinese philosophy, Xin signifies the human "heart-mind." This perception is in line with recent scientific findings that the "thought" process involves the entire body, not just the brain analyzing sensory data. Xin is also called the Yang Fire Mind.

Yi Mind

The Yi Mind is also considered to be a "mind," but this is the calm, steadfast, wisdom mind. Its main focus is to lead and control the Xin Mind, and when this dominance occurs successfully, your will and intentions will be steadfast. Yi Mind is also called the Yin Water Mind.

Qi Energy

Qi refers to the vital life force or energy that flows within and around all living things. The goal with cultivating the Qi is to build up a reservoir of Qi energy in the lower dan tien to nourish the body. How that Qi energy is manifested directly impacts the body's Yin and Yang balance. Qi energy is classified as either Fire (Yang) or Water (Yin).

When Qi is excessive, the body is too Yang. When Qi is deficient, the body is too Yin. If too Yang, the Qi is fiery, causing body to heat up and creating emotional instability in the mind, making it scattered and confused. It is called "Fire Qi." In contrast, a body deficient in Qi energy becomes too Yin and illness results. Therefore, the overarching intent of both Tai Chi Chuan and Qigong is to build up and then maintain, a strong, balanced state of Qi energy within the body.

The Theory of How Yin and Yang Function

The constant and dynamic interplay of nature's forces is demonstrated in a multitude of ways. As nature strives for balance between matter and force, the energetic interaction frequently manifests in spirals. This spiraling action is a key characteristic of this interplay between forces. Such spirals exist in galaxies, tornadoes, seashells, DNA's double helix twisted strand, and even in water circling a drain.

The Yin and Yang symbol is only a two-dimensional representation of these natural forces' interaction. The symbol itself is a flat circle. However, the action created by actual Yin-Yang interplay manifests in a spiral. Spirals are continuously evolving perfect circles that increase or diminish in size. Every movement in Tai Chi Chuan is based on these ever-changing, spiraling circles. That spiraling circle concept is an important thing to understand about Tai Chi Chuan.

Lau Tzu, the revered Chinese sage, emphasized the need to

embrace the ever-changing and opposing nature of the Yin and Yang forces. He wrote that if one has the "wish to close it, must first open it; wish to weaken it, must first strengthen it; wish to abolish it, must first raise it; wish to take it, must first offer it." Also, Tai Chi Chuan classical philosophy says, "withdrawing is releasing, and releasing is withdrawing."

Tai Chi Chuan is rooted in the theory of Yin-Yang. By striving for a deeper level of understanding, you will see that there are endless ways to apply this concept in many areas of your life. The theory is the foundation of the art while Tai Chi Chuan's movements are the theory's application. Once you understand the theory, you can apply it to experience Tai Chi Chuan's substantial and insubstantial essence – using nature's interplay of forces. Whether your goal is to attain a high level of martial skill or use these strategies in other areas of life, you will have gained a tool that many lack.

Application of Yin-Yang Theory

Remembering Yin and Yang and the spiral resulting from their interplay is an effective way to view and learn Tai Chi Chuan's basic skills. Remember, the lower dan tien, that Qi storage space that also houses your Wuji stillness? It is from this Wuji center that Qi energy is stored and from where Tai Chi Chuan's spiraling movements are initiated.

In the practice of Tai Chi Chuan, the interplay between Yin and Yang is a dynamic and ever-changing relationship, encompassing a wide range of opposing movements such as offensive and defensive, falling and rising, coming and going, entering and exiting, and releasing and withdrawing, to name a few. Each opposing movement is an integral part of a unified whole.

When learning Tai Chi Chuan, always keep in mind the dynamic and constant interplay between Yin and Yang within each movement of the set. That interplay is creating a fluid, ever-changing situation internally, with each movement working like a pump, building Qi energy and circulating it throughout the body.

This same constant interplay takes place in martial applications as well. For example, in a combat situation, there can be a swift transition from bending in a Yang offense, such as an arm lock, to extending defensively in a Yin withdrawal. Similarly, a rising of the body in a Yang substantial action can immediately transition into falling of the body in a Yin insubstantial movement. At all times, there must be an awareness and flexibility that is instantly and unexpectedly responsive to the immediate situation.

Recognizing that Yin and Yang are parts of a whole will give your practice new significance and power. This is because you will have a better understanding of the underlying purpose of each movement which, in turn, leads to a more effective practice. Your Tai Chi set will steadily increase your Qi energy and improve its flow throughout your body. It will strengthen and calm your Yi-Xin mind so that you can solve life's problems more effectively. Similarly, a deep understanding of the overall nature of Yin and Yang will enable you to improve and evolve your martial arts skills, making you a formidable opponent.

Qigong Practice Definitions, Theory, and Applications

Qigong is a mind-body-spirit practice. The name translates as "cultivated energy." Qi means the life force, while Gong means awareness gained through practice. Qigong's purpose is to improve mental and physical health. It does so by gently aligning posture, movement, breath, and intent. There are thousands of Qigong practices – far too many to detail here. All of them, however, adopt the principles that underlie Tai Chi Chuan described above. In addition, there are three other aspects incorporated into Qigong theory. These are Kan, Li, and Shen. Consider these to be the methods one can use to achieve Yin and Yang's positive results. These three aspects are defined below.

Kan

Kan has a water essence and is a means used to cool the body down and make the individual more Yin. It, along with Li, is used to balance and control the outcome of the Yin and Yang interaction.

Li

Li has a fire essence. Li is used to activate the body, making it more Yang. It, along with Kan, is used to balance and control the outcome of the Yin and Yang interaction.

Shen

The Shen comes from a Chinese word that encompasses all that westerners call "god," "spirit," "soul," or "immortal." Qigong practitioners believe the Shen is responsible for consciousness, cognition, emotions, and our fundamental essence. In the real world, the Shen thinks, plans, and feels. Qigong theory believes that the Shen encompasses both the Yi and Xin minds.

It is considered spirit, one's higher nature, which is in contact with the divine nature. When you are in harmony with your Shen, you are in harmony with yourself and everything around you. According to traditional Chinese thought, the Shen presides over the activities that take place on the mental, spiritual, and creative planes. The Shen does not contain either Kan water or Li fire aspects. Rather, Shen is able to make Kan and Li's effects more powerful.

Qigong Theory

Qigong holds that too much of either the Yin or Yang energy is detrimental. Instead, the goal of the practice is to balance these energies so that the body functions harmoniously.

One of the most important goals of Qigong practice is learning the use of Kan (water) and Li (fire) mechanisms to control the outcome of the Yin and Yang interactions. Although Kan-Li are related to Yin-Yang, they are not the same thing as Yin and Yang. This idea of Kan and Li has been studied by Qigong practitioners for hundreds of years. They believe that once we learn how to use Kan and Li mechanisms correctly, Yin and Yang will be equalized and exist harmoniously.

Unless one is sick or malnourished, Qigong practitioners generally believe that the body is too Yang, the effect of which is that excess Yang causes the body to burn out and age faster. Therefore, Qigong uses Kan (water) to cool the body down, thereby slowing the aging process and lengthening life. Much of Qigong practice aims at improving and increasing the quality and quantity of Kan water essence in the body and reduce the body quantity of Li fire essence. Success in this endeavor means the acquisition of healthier, clearer thoughts, and stronger focus. This, in turn, leads to an increase in awareness that enhances the ability to learn and apply yielding skills. The process has a synergetic effect because, a higher level of yielding awareness makes it easier to use Kan and Li to regulate the Qi of the Yin-Yang energies.

We have addressed the Kan and Li theory. Next comes the theory behind Shen (spirit) which relates directly to both the Yi and Xin minds of Tai Chi Chuan and Qigong's additional Kan and Li aspects. The Kan and Li aspects are closely related to the Yi and Xin minds (hereafter the Yi-Xin mind). The two minds can be considered in tandem because their functions are inseparably entwined. Although the logical Yi mind strives to control the emotional Xin mind, it also utilizes the emotional and creative perceptions of the Xin mind when deciding what action to take. In both Qigong and Tai Chi, the Yi-Xin mind functions like a battlefield general determining and directing the strategies to be used.

The Shen spirit is something more – something "bigger." It is overarching, functioning like an all-knowing entity in charge of the general, officers, and soldiers' morale. If the Shen is high, many things can be accomplished. Throughout history, superior forces have been defeated by the inferior forces because of insufficient knowledge and lower morale. In Qigong, the cultivation of the Shen spirit is crucial to the success of one's practice. The goal is to raise and balance your Shen spirit without getting too emotional or excited. The Yi-Xin mind has the task of raising the Shen spirit. When the Shen is strong, the mind is clear, focused, and able to fully engage in the training or practice. This helps enhance physical performance as well as mental and emotional well-being. Additionally, when the Shen is strong, the practitioner is able to execute strategies with precision, as they are able to remain calm and focused, even in the midst of challenges or distractions. Qigong training focuses on keeping the Shen spirit high. Maintaining a high level of Shen spirit will enable you to become proficient at regulating Kan and Li.

Bodhidharma, also known as Da Mo, believed that the harmony between the Shen spirit and Qi energy is essential for a long and peaceful life. He said:

> "If one does not keep the mother (Qi) and the son (Shen spirit) together, though Qi breathes internally, Spirit is labored and craves the external, so the spirit is always dirty and not clear. If Shen is not clear, the original harmonious Qi will disperse gradually, and they cannot be kept together."

So, achieving the ability to regulate the Shen spirit, is essential for anyone hoping to reach high levels of Qigong practice.

Applying Qigong Theory

As stated, many times, breath leads the body's Qi energy. Slow breathing calms and steadies the Qi flow while rapid breathing energizes it. When the body is active or agitated, it exhales longer than it inhales, making the body more Yang. This breathing change leads Qi to the skin where sweat releases its excess energy. By contrast, the longer inhales that accompany sadness or a distraught state lead the Qi inward – making the body more Yin and creating a sense of coldness.

Maintaining a balanced breathing pattern is crucial for ensuring that the Yin and Yang energies remain in harmony. When the inhale and exhale are of equal duration, the Kan water and Li fire aspects of breathing are balanced, and the flow of Qi energy throughout the body is optimal. Inhaling, the Kan water activity, draws the Qi inward and lowers the body's Yang energy, while exhaling, the Li fire activity, directs the Qi outward and through the muscles and tendons, increasing the body's Yang energy. However, an excessive level of Yang energy can be exhausting and lead to various physical and mental issues. Therefore, it is essential to maintain a balanced breathing pattern to achieve a healthy equilibrium of Yin and Yang energies.

A longer exhale leads the Qi outward toward the five extremities, and this can help increase energy and excitement. These five extremities – including the crown, the two Lao Gong cavities in the center of the palms, and the two Yong Quan cavities at the bottom of the feet – can make you more conscious of, and better able to interact with, your surroundings.

In Qigong, the combined Yi-Xin mind is even more important than the breathing pattern, because it controls and directs the body's Kan water and Li fire aspects. It is the Yi-Xin mind that decides whether the body needs to inhale longer to increase the Kan water aspect of the Qi's energy or whether the body needs to exhale longer so as to increase the body's Li or fire Qi energy. These decisions, in turn, ultimately determine the body's overall Yin-Yang balance.

The Yi-Xin mind also determines the level of Shen spirit within the body by increasing its level of positive thinking. Increased Qi energy to the mind increases positive thoughts. The Shen spirit strengthens as the mind's positive thoughts increase and predominate.

Qigong practices, however, go beyond focusing on the body's internal workings. They also seek connectedness to the external environment. This seeking for connectivity applies to relationships between people as well. If we use the mechanism of Kan and Li breathing for balance, that same sense of balance affects our relationships with other people. It allows us to remain calm and steady. At the same time, it allows others to more easily interact with our rooted, authentic being.

According to Qigong, the ability to control the mind and the breathing are the two primary ways to increase and direct Qi to achieve a balance of the body's Yin and Yang energies. The workings of the mind and the breathing are inseparable. When one's mental state is harmonious, the breath will be too. Conversely, when one has control over their breathing, their mind is able to achieve deeper levels of focus and harmony.

Qigong and Health

Achieving better health is a primary goal of Qigong practice. Qigong practitioners believe that immediate resort to pharmaceuticals is not the best way to cure illness. The Qigong approach is to solve the problem at its root. In the absence of modern chemistry, ancient Chinese medicine turned to the approach of balancing the body's Qi energies, using Kan and Li's fire and water mechanisms. Some of that ancient medical knowledge is being revisited today.

Arthritis serves as a notable example. In modern times, many individuals with arthritis rely on pharmaceutical drugs to alleviate their pain. While these medications can provide temporary relief, they do not address the underlying issue or provide a long-term cure. In contrast, using Qigong as a means to treat arthritis often offers a more comprehensive and sustainable approach.

Qigong exercises specifically target the rebuilding of joint strength, aiding in the restoration of mobility and function. The slow, deliberate movements of Qigong also contribute to improved circulation throughout the body, effectively massaging the affected areas. By promoting a harmonious balance between Yin and Yang energies within the body, Qigong facilitates the repair of damaged tissues and joints.

The beauty of the Qigong approach lies in its focus on addressing the root cause of arthritis, rather than solely alleviating symptoms with medication. This holistic approach not only reduces reliance on drugs but also promotes overall health and longevity by restoring the body's natural healing abilities.

A quick search on platforms like Google will yield numerous articles and studies that highlight the effectiveness of Qigong in treating arthritis. The abundance of research and positive testimonials further validate the benefits of integrating Qigong into arthritis management strategies.

Modern medical practices indeed incorporate principles that align with the concepts of Kan and Li. In both Eastern and Western medical theories, the ultimate goal of healing is to restore balance within the body. This balance can be achieved through various methods, including the application of cold therapy and the use of ice to reduce fever and swelling, respectively. From the perspective of Qigong theory, the concepts of Kan (water) and Li (fire) play a vital role in understanding the quantity and circulation of Qi, the vital energy within the body. By regulating these energies, practitioners can strengthen, improve, and maintain their overall health.

Cold therapy, such as applying cold compresses or using ice packs, is often employed to lower body temperature and reduce fever. This aligns with the principle of Kan, representing the water element. By reducing excess heat, the body's balance is restored, allowing it to function optimally. Similarly, the use of ice to reduce swelling caused by injuries corresponds to the concept of Li, representing the fire element. By applying cold to the affected area, the circulation of Qi is regulated, reducing inflammation and promoting healing.

It is also important to acknowledge the Chinese medical art of acupuncture. Acupuncture's varied use of the body's energy pathways to balance the body's Yin and Yang energies has helped millions. It is one of the first Chinese-based medical alternatives to be incorporated into the practices of Western-trained medical doctors, including those practicing at the famed Mayo Clinic.

The theoretical foundation underlying acupuncture and other Chinese medical approaches is called the Five Elements – or Five Phases – theory. This theoretical construct describes the interplay of the natural forces that Chinese medicine believes determine a person's physical and mental health. The theory is quite extensive in its analysis and somewhat outside the purview of this book. It does, however, provide guidance applicable to yielding skills. Many yielding practitioners use the Five Element / Phase theory to enhance their awareness and understanding of other people's motivations, thoughts, and actions. Moreover, every single martial arts master with whom I have studied has emphasized the importance of understanding and using the Five Element / Phase theory. For that reason, a discussion of the Five Element / Phase theory is included as Appendix A to this book.

Final Thoughts

There are six primary concepts underlying the practices of Tai Chi Chuan and Qigong. These are fundamental to the student's goal of leading the body's Qi to create optimal physical and mental health. Please keep the following concepts in mind as you undertake your yielding journey:

1. The buildup and leading of Qi is of paramount importance to both practices. As noted previously, the lower dan tien (defined and described earlier in this chapter), increases and stores Qi energy. It also releases Qi energy to travel throughout the body. This action is triggered by the Yi-Xin mind, which sends its intent through the spinal cord to the lower dan tien. At that point, Qi is released and led to carry out the intent. When there is an abundance of Qi stored in the lower dan tien, the life force becomes strong. If it is

deficient, the life force is weak and the body subject to illness.

2. The body has the ability to store unlimited amounts of Qi energy. Chinese theory believes Qi can also be stored in eight additional reservoirs. When Qi becomes abundant in the lower dan tien, it will begin to circulate into these eight reservoirs, sometimes called the Eight Vessels. The Small Circulation meditation is a crucial practice for boosting Qi and promoting its circulation throughout the body, as well as filling the Eight Vessels. You will learn more about the Small Circulation in Chapter 10.

3. Strive to circulate the Qi energy smoothly. When the Qi is abundant throughout the body, it becomes easy for it to strengthen and nourish the life force. To reach this goal of smoothly circulating Qi energy, Yin and Yang need to be balanced.

4. Cultivate an emotionally neutral mind. In Qigong, one goal is to learn how to use the Yi mind to regulate the emotional Xin mind. Controlling the emotional Xin mind is essential to finding Yin-Yang balance. It is essential to free yourself from uncontrolled emotional bondage if you want to experience the 4-Hs of Qigong: health, humility, harmony, and happiness.

5. Raise up your Shen spirit. When the Shen spirit has vitality, our life force becomes strong. This starts by our building up the Qi in the lower dan tien. This has the effect of energizing our Yi-Xin mind, allowing it to nourish and raise the spirit.

6. Reflect on the meaning of life. Analyze your life and your training with an open mind. Seek to discover your unrealized potentials. Without reaching an understanding of life's meaning and your own place in it, you will be left wandering and confused, subject to depression and low self-esteem. Form goals based on

your newly acquired understandings, bringing purpose to your actions and gaining the momentum needed to accomplish whatever you set out to do.

If you come to the Northwest Fighting Arts' Academy and want to learn Tai Chi Chuan and Qigong, one of the first things we will ask about is your main objectives and what areas in your life feel deficient. With that information, we can work with you to build a plan going forward.

Everyone's Tai Chi and Qigong practice is unique. If you have a career that is demanding and stressful, I would want you to incorporate more Yin-oriented practices to help settle your Qi and keep you rooted. If you were coming here after spending time in chemotherapy, I would recommend doing more Yang-oriented approaches to help build up your immune system to bring balance. Always, we are looking for ways to find harmony using the Kan water and Li fire mechanisms to channel Qi and ultimately balance your Yin and Yang forces. This will lead to a fruitful life lived outside of the realm of extremes.

PART III

STRATEGIES FOR DEVELOPING A PERSONALIZED YIELDING PRACTICE

9

MEDITATIONS THAT DEVELOP HIGHER LEVELS OF YIELDING

There are many meditative practices we can use to develop higher levels of awareness, leading to an improved ability to implement yielding concepts in all areas of our lives. In this section, I break down some of the strategies and techniques that will take your yielding skill set to the next level. As you read through these different methods, it is important to keep it simple. Taking on too much or trying techniques that are too advanced will not have good results. Being disciplined enough to maintain consistency is essential to success. Consistent practice is necessary to experience the greatest amount of success. Lastly, try to keep it fun, interesting, and inspiring. If you are enjoying the practice, everything else will seem to fall in place.

As you start to learn about some of these different methods, remember that the intent is to create both ritual and active practices for use during daily activities. I recommend starting with a single ritual practice that you stick with for at least three months or longer. As stated previously, ritual practices are the root of any meditative practice. I always tell new students that they should commit to at least fifteen to twenty minutes a day to ritual practice. This consistency is probably the most important lesson to learn in any meditative art. Often times it takes many repetitions and hundreds of hours of effort to see what these methods are trying to teach us. Bouncing around, from one thing to the next means never reaching any depth in the practice. Bruce Lee once said: "I do not fear the man who knows ten thousand kicks, I fear the man who has done one kick ten thousand times."

If, however, you spend a considerable amount of time practicing a particular method but feel like it is just not resonating with you, move on and try another. You do want to enjoy the practice. Maybe you are just not ready for the one you were doing. You can always return to it at another time. If it is feeling good to you, staying with it for years will help you to reach levels of awareness and skill most people will never experience.

Overview of Meditation Methods

There are four meditation approaches to consider when selecting and developing your ritual practice. These are as follows.

Daily Resets

These are incredibly simple and easy to use meditation tools for everyone, no matter what their goals are with meditation. These powerful resets can be done anywhere in as little as two to three minutes and yield a variety of positive outcomes. Some resets generate energy, spark creative juices, or focus the mind.

Performance Rituals

These are derived from a variety of methods to help you focus and bring you to the energy level you need in order to perform your best. Whether you are an athlete, speaker, musician, or actor, if you seek optimal performance in an activity, performance rituals will help you to achieve your ultimate potential. These rituals involve the use of different breathing strategies and physical movements, as well as visual and auditory visualizations, all of which help you focus, put you in a present state of mind, and give you the ability to reach higher levels of success.

Nightly Routines

These are often used for exploring dreamwork, seeking creative inspiration, or overcoming insomnia. Nightly sessions will involve visualizations, breathing strategies, mental programming, and sometimes, movement.

Morning Routines

These are an important foundation for building a deep spiritual meditation practice. These meditation rituals will vary depending on your goals and desired results. Some of the meditation techniques you might use in a morning routine are still meditations, such as sitting, standing, and lying, combined with many different breathing strategies, as well as moving meditations, such as Tai Chi, Qigong, walking stretching, partner sets, and physical breathing exercises.

As you start your practice, you can pick which of these methods will help you achieve your desired results most efficiently with the time and resources you currently have available. Before diving into the specific mediation methods, there are three preliminary tasks to undertake:

1. Adopt a mindset and plan
2. Initiate a visualization regime
3. Learn the attitudinal keys that will make your meditation practice successful

Using a Nine-Point Plan to Develop a Successful Mindset and Plan Your Practice

There are certain practices you can undertake that will enable you to be successful in creating and maintaining your practice. These practices can be summarized as follows:

1. **Log your meditation sessions:** Plan on logging your meditation sessions either in a journal, on your phone, or on your computer. Keeping a record will help when looking back and evaluating your progress. In addition, the simple act of writing down your accomplishments offers you a mental reward.
2. **Schedule your practice sessions:** Designating a specific time each day when you will not be distracted or interrupted will dramatically accelerate your success.
3. **Keep a journal of ideas and inspirations:** This will help you stay on track and also offer a visual reward to help keep you motivated and consistent. It is also a great tool for reaching new insights and creative inspirations. A journal can also help you discover patterns that will allow you to recognize different perspectives and experience more profound levels of awareness.
4. **Use positive incentives:** Implementing positive incentives will help you keep a consistent, grounded meditation practice. Examples of using a positive incentive might be something like donating $20 to your favorite charity every time you miss one of your scheduled sessions.
5. **Seek out support:** Finding support and ongoing education will guide you and keep you moving forward with fewer distractions. You can attend a local class or meditation group or seek out a teacher or program such as the Academy's Online Program at https://portland-

taichiacademy.com/online-training/. Life is short – help is available.

6. **Create a meditation list:** To begin developing your meditation plan, start by making a list of all of the meditation strategies that sound helpful for achieving your desired outcomes. Once you have this list, evaluate your current lifestyle and schedule to see which practice will be easiest to implement. Start small. Begin with just one of the meditation practices on your list. Do it consistently, until it is successful and becomes part of your life. Keep in mind the next couple of meditation strategies you want to implement. Meditation strategies often build on each other and having a clear understanding of how you look to grow your practice will help keep you focused.

7. **Break negative habits:** Many of our habitual thought patterns are negative. Use meditation to break these negative habits and acquire the tools you need to increase positive thoughts and achieve positive momentum. Having strong positive momentum counteracts the tendency toward procrastination. Being confident and decisive will enable you to follow through and achieve the things in life that are important to you.

8. **Create patterns:** It is important to create patterns and habits that work toward achieving success. An upcoming section, Understanding the Ten Essential Keys to Success, discusses how to create patterns and use them to assist you with your meditation practice.

9. **Learn how to use a visualization practice:** Visualization and imagery are used in three ways: for internal visualizations, for external visualizations, and to aid in goal setting.

Understanding Visualization Strategies

Visualization practice is a necessary component of most meditation practices. Without a heightened level of concentration, no one would be successful with visualization or mental imagery. Therefore, to boost concentration, you should determine a specific time you will practice. Having a steady, dependable practice will help you focus your energy, yielding better results. When setting these practice times, also keep in mind the need to set a time limit for yourself. Without a time limit, distractions can creep in. Additionally, make sure you are getting enough rest – this is a critical requirement for enhanced visualization sessions, because if you are tired, it is extremely difficult to maintain a deep level of concentration.

Yielding teaches you three main visualization strategies: internal, external, and imagining goals. Your training list or blueprint may not use all or any of these particular techniques as a primary focus in the beginning, but it is good to know these tools exist as a resource for future use.

Internal visualizations can be utilized by visualizing positive emotional states, relaxation, reduced stress, or improved energy. This type of visualization can help you tap into energy areas in the body such as the lungs or kidneys, which will additionally help circulate energy in the body. As you improve, you'll learn to store this energy and guide it to necessary locations for healing.

On the other hand, external visualizations can be used to ground your mental state in the present moment. If you are looking to improve your golf swing, for example, or have increased charisma in a work presentation, visualize yourself being successful in these endeavors. Doing so will help you strategize how to improve on your daily activities. This visualization can also be used to picture your goals, keeping you accountable and on a path to success with clear, specific goals in mind.

Understanding the Ten Essential Keys to Success

There are certain attitudes and mindsets that will enable you to achieve success in whatever endeavor you undertake. The ten most important of these are the following:

1. **Knowing yourself through meditation:** This is important because it cultivates self-awareness, insight, and understanding. By observing your thoughts, emotions, and patterns of behavior without judgment, you gain clarity about your true nature, desires, and limitations. This self-knowledge empowers you to make conscious choices, develop emotional resilience, and align your actions with your values. Through meditation, you can uncover deeper layers of self-discovery, fostering personal growth, and enhancing overall well-being.
2. **Develop and maintain positive self-esteem and a positive self-image:** This is crucial for achieving your goals. If you believe you are smart enough and good enough to achieve success, then you have positive self-esteem. Visualize yourself as someone who can easily do what you want to do. This can help you develop a positive self-image.
3. **Understand your intention:** Knowing why you want to achieve what you want to achieve provides clarity and motivation, helping you stay focused and determined. It helps you understand the purpose behind your actions, and it gives you a sense of direction and meaning. Having a clear and compelling reason for pursuing a goal also helps you overcome obstacles and setbacks, as it reminds you of the bigger picture and why you started in the first place.
4. **Imagine your desired outcome as often as possible:** The ability to have a clear, precise vision of what you

desire will help you carry out your vision, both physically and mentally. All of humanity's great accomplishments began as a vision.

5. **Determination is essential:** Possessing a strong will can help you to overcome many challenges, weaknesses, or limitations that you may encounter.
6. **Be confident:** If you do not believe in your ability to make something happen, chances are you will fail. Initially, having a "Yes, I can" attitude will give you momentum and help build your confidence. To reach higher levels of confidence, you must grow, learn, practice, study, try, and fail and try again and succeed. Trying, failing, trying again, and then succeeding, builds confidence and resilience. In psychology, this concept is often referred to as the confidence / competence loop. Without confidence, we revert to fear. When we are fearful, it is difficult to take action. Fear leads to procrastination and slows growth. Once you let go of fear, it becomes easier to take action. The best way to become more confident is to become more competent.
7. **Enjoy the process of change!** A strong belief in what you are doing will give you the energy to grow and become successful. Learning how to enjoy the tasks needed to accomplish your goals will help you stay on track and follow through with what is required to get you where you want to go.
8. **Learn what you must:** Often, many of our goals do not fall within our natural abilities or current level of knowledge. You must strive to learn whatever is necessary to accomplish the tasks that are needed to achieve your goal.
9. **Keep problems and setbacks in perspective:** How well you successfully move forward toward goals is often connected to how well you can act and react when problems arise. Mistakes and setbacks are sure to come,

and they may delay your progress. Do not let this distract you. Stay focused and remember your purpose; it will help you stay strong. Remain optimistic throughout setbacks and weakened emotional states. With practice, desire and determination grow, and overcoming setbacks becomes easier.

10. **Appreciate your success and enjoy the satisfaction of your accomplishments:** Once you reach a goal, there is often a tendency to forget all the steps and emotional hurdles you overcame to succeed. One of the most important requirements for making your new habits and changes part of who you are is to pay attention and appreciate what it took to reach your goal. Enjoy the end results. Appreciate the rewards. Acknowledge your success. Reflect on your efforts and how you overcame all of the setbacks and hurdles along the way.

Meditation Resets

The first meditation tool – and one of the most important tools you will learn – is the reset. Resets are used to help keep you in tune throughout the day. They are considered active meditations. It is easy to let the day pass by with no effort made to improve your physical or mental well-being. Use resets to keep up with your busy schedule and grow your meditation practice at the same time.

Although it may seem frequent, these resets are best when performed every hour to ninety minutes. The resets are quick and simple (completed in as little as two to three minutes), can be performed anywhere, and will not disrupt your daily routine. There are three types of resets that I recommend and are listed below:

- **Still resets:** breathing routines, sounds, energetic circulations, and internal movements

- **Movement resets:** walking, forms, standing, and sitting movements
- **Philosophical resets:** visualizations, repeated phrases, and emotional reprogramming

Still Meditation Resets

The Inner Smile Meditation

You can manage your level of enjoyment and ease throughout the day using this activity. The best way to start this practice is as a meditation, but the ultimate goal is to incorporate it into your regular routine. It will become simple to perform this practice anywhere and can be used as a mental reset once you have gone through the procedures a sufficient number of times. Your ultimate goal is to subconsciously practice the inner smile. The advantages of this practice will become most apparent at this time. It is a straightforward meditation that has remarkable effects on relaxation, stress release, and tension relief. The energetic shift is sufficient justification for incorporating this practice into your day. The intention behind a smile warms the body and mind, putting you in a better frame of mind. After all, it's nearly impossible to have a genuine smile without a resulting sensation of happiness.

To get started, try sitting in a comfortable position with good posture. Take a few deep breaths just to become more present. Now with a soft intent, visualize softly smiling with the back of your throat. Notice the energetic shift in your body, mind, and spirit. It may be subtle for some, more profound for others, but you will notice a shift. Imagine if you did this as often as you could every day and it became a habit. What if 80 to 90 percent of the time you were walking around with this feeling of ease and positivity? This one simple practice can change your life dramatically.

To begin a more in-depth practice of the inner smile, sit in a comfortable position, and again take a few deep breaths, becoming more present. Start by lightly smiling with your mouth. Let your face soften and feel the smile. If this is difficult, think of a time in your life when you were happy or of someone who makes you feel good. Once you have this image in your mind, think about the ease and emotional peace you felt during that point in your life or how you feel when you are with someone who brings you happiness. Having this ability to clearly visualize yourself in a moment of happiness you once experienced is very helpful. You want to be genuine with your smile and the emotion behind the smile in order to get the most out of this practice.

Now smile with your eyes and lightly lift the crown of your head. Move the smile to the back of your throat, keeping your jaw and tongue relaxed. As you start to become mentally at ease, let the smile sink down your throat into your heart; feel a sense of openness, love, joy, and happiness. Continue the smile down through all of your organs and reproductive system. For the next two to three breaths at least, expand your awareness by watching this smile radiate in your body. You can use this practice as a short reset throughout your day or you can use it for an extended meditation. Finish by letting this positive, relaxed energy move to your lower dan tien or navel center.

Lung Breathing

This a valuable tool for keeping the lungs strong and healthy. The average adult has a total lung capacity of approximately six thousand cubic centimeters. But at rest, the average adult uses only three hundred to five hundred cubic centimeters of that potential. So, if you are not active, over time your lungs can become weak and brittle. Just like your muscles, if you do not use your lungs, they will begin to shrink and become weak, and you will be more prone to illness. If you are frequently in an environment that puts you in still positions for long periods of time, it is extremely important for your health to consciously spend time performing lung exercises.

With this exercise, you will focus on breathing into every part of the lungs. First, you will focus on breathing into the front side of the lungs. For this exercise, start by sitting or standing in a comfortable position, then gently round your shoulders and spine forward. You should feel a subtle stretch across your back. This position will also lightly stretch the backside of the lungs, while simultaneously softening the front side of the lungs. Now that the front side of the lungs is relaxed, breathe deeply at least six to twelve times. Notice how the front side of your body expands and contracts. You are exercising the front sides of the lungs.

Next, you will focus on breathing into the backside of the lungs. As before, sit or stand in a comfortable position. Then do a soft backward arch with the spine while rolling the shoulders back. Be sure to not arch so far that you feel tight; this should be a relaxed position. Now breathe deeply, focusing on the back sides of the lungs. Again, take at least six to twelve deep, full breaths as you practice this position.

To exercise the sides of the lungs, we will use the same strategy. Softly lean to your left, stretching the right side of your body and lightly softening the left side of your body. Then breathe deeply into the left side, six to twelve times, focusing on your lungs expanding and contracting with the breath on the left side. Repeat for the right side.

If you are having difficulty visualizing this breathing strategy, close your eyes and bring your awareness inward. Watch your lungs stretch and relax with every breath.

Spinal Rotations

These are essential practices for maintaining overall health and cultivating energy. Even though there will be a small amount of physical movement when performing this technique, we will use this as a still reset. This reset should be used every day to enhance your awareness of the spine and make it easier for you to practice many of the energetic movements we will be using later. Having a healthy spine will build your energy and heighten your intuition.

You can practice this exercise sitting or standing. When first starting this practice, a good way to increase your control and awareness, and to get off to a good start, is to use "the pressure method." This is easiest to do with a partner. Have your partner press on each vertebra, starting at the tailbone and working all the way up to the base of the skull. As they pause on each vertebra along the spine, try to move just that one small piece of the spine, coordinating this movement with one or two breaths, or until you can isolate this area. This will help you to develop sensitivity along the spine and soon you will have good control of your spine and the ability to move it freely. Once you have practiced the pressure method and have good awareness and control of your spine, you can begin practicing spinal rotations.

Spinal rotations can be practiced while sitting or standing. The body itself moves very little, which is why this exercise is a still reset. Begin by visualizing a soft, light wave traveling up the spine, moving one vertebra at a time. The wave is moving in three dimensions: up and down, front and back, and left and right. Remember, for this practice, it is a very subtle movement. As you develop better control and more sensitivity, you will find this very refreshing. It is a great practice to do as often as possible. To develop coordination in this practice, it is not essential that the breath follow the movement. You may find, however, that it feels natural to inhale as the soft wave travels up the spine and exhale as you sink and relax.

Rapid Breath

This is used in the Chinese martial arts for generating powerful strikes and focusing energy on different areas in the body. It is also used by yoga practitioners. They refer to it as Kapalabhati or "skull shining" breath. This practice is intended for cleaning the cranial sinuses but also has many other effects such as directing energy, generating power, increasing awareness, energizing the mind, releasing stress and toxins from the body, and curing anemia.

Rapid breath can be used as a charging reset. It is best

performed sitting or standing. You will be using your nose to breathe rapidly, in and out, for sets of thirty full breaths. As you transition between sets, take three deep and normal breaths. Alternate between rapid breath sets and relaxed breath sets for two to three minutes. As you do so, inhale as much air as possible, keeping balance with your breath. Your stomach should draw into your body with force, exhaling air from your nose powerfully and then expanding quickly to pull in the next breath. It will take some time to be able to relax and have a smooth rhythm. Be consistent and soon you will be able to perform rapid breath for longer periods of time or increase the number of repetitions in each set.

The Six Healing Sounds

The six healing sounds are simple to implement and initiate a powerful source of healing and gaining mental strength. When practicing the six healing sounds, it is good to perform them as a sitting meditation during ritual practice. This will give you the focus needed to develop a strong practice. After building a good foundation with the sounds and mental visualizations, you can perform them anywhere and in any position as well as use them for active practices. This will give you the freedom to experience the many benefits that come from this training.

Start with a comfortable sitting posture, with good alignment, and relax your breath. Let the backs of your hands rest lightly on your thighs. Take at least three breaths to find your center and to focus. Softly smile with the back of your throat and let that smile sink down through your body, letting go of any tension in your body.

Lungs Sound

Begin with a slow inhale as you raise your arms slowly in front of your body. When your arms reach your upper dan tien, or about eye level, rotate your palms, turning them outward. Continue moving your arms upward as you exhale until they are directly over your head. Your fingers will be pointing toward each other, palms facing upward, and your arms will be softly rounded as if you were reaching around a large beach ball.

Lightly close your jaws so that your teeth softly touch, then open your lips. Open your eyes wide as you inhale and look up, expanding up and outward with your arms. Softly and slowly exhale through your teeth, making the *SSSSSSS* sound with your tongue resting behind your teeth. This sound can be practiced both audibly and subvocally. After performing the sound, inhale, and bring your head back to a neutral, relaxed position. On your next exhale, look up and repeat the sound again.

Visualize heat in your lungs and let all of the sadness, sorrow, depression, grief, and negative energy be expelled from your lungs as they softly compress. This practice will help alleviate sadness, depression, sickness, asthma, and emphysema. Perform the sound at least six times, or as many as you like.

On your last repetition, slowly lower your arms, letting your hands rest softly, palms facing upward, on your thighs. Close your eyes and visualize your lungs as healthy and active. Picture a bright, white light filling your lungs and radiating throughout your body. With each breath, feel the exchange of cool, fresh energy replacing the hot energy in your lungs. In Chinese medicine, the lungs are commonly associated with the large intestine, the color white, the element of metal, and the season of fall. The negative emotions associated with the lungs are grief, sadness, and depression. The positive emotions are courage and righteousness.

Kidneys Sound

This sound can be performed either sitting in a chair with your knees and ankles together or sitting on your heels with your shins on the floor and knees together. As with the lungs sound, begin by lightly smiling in the back of your throat and sinking this smile down to your kidneys. Be sure to maintain a good, upright alignment with your posture. Take a deep, relaxed breath, and as you exhale, place your hands around your knees. Push your lower back to the rear, letting your arms straighten and your spine softly round. This will feel as if you are pushing your kidneys out the small of your back. As you are pulling your arms straight, lift your head and look straight ahead. Make a WOOOOOO sound, as you round your lips and exhale softly as if you were blowing out a candle. When you exhale lightly, contract your abdomen and bring it in toward your kidneys. Visualize the excess fear, heat, wet, and sick energies squeezing out of the fascia surrounding your kidneys. Inhale and lightly relax, expanding your abdomen and slowly straightening your spine. Repeat.

After you have finished with each sound, rest, and visualize your positive efforts. Straighten your spine and relax your legs. Reset your hands, palms up, on your thighs. Bring your awareness into your kidneys by closing your eyes and breathing into your lower back area. Picture a blue color filling your kidneys as you smile into your kidneys. Imagine you are still making the kidney sound. Repeat at least six times. In traditional Chinese medicine, the kidneys are considered one of the vital organs and are associated with the water element, the color black or dark blue, the emotion of fear, and the season of winter. The kidneys are also believed to govern the bones, produce marrow, and regulate the reproductive and urinary systems. The bladder, which is associated with the kidneys, is responsible for storing and eliminating urine. Fear is the emotion that is traditionally associated with the kidneys. The positive emotion is gentleness.

Liver Sound

This sound is performed in a comfortable sitting position with good alignment. Visualize your liver and smile into it. When you feel as if you have made a good connection with your liver, slowly move your arms up and out to the sides, palms up. Breathe in deeply while slowly raising your arms over your head. Follow this upward movement with your eyes. Interlace your fingers, then slowly turn your palms up toward the sky. As you are slightly leaning to the left, stretch your palms up and slowly over to the left in a light, easy stretch, gently pulling on your liver.

Now open your eyes wide and exhale the liver sound *SHHHHHH*. Your eyes are considered the openings of the liver. Opening your eyes wide will let your liver expel negative energies. As you are making the sound, let all the excess heat and anger leave your liver and the fascia surrounding it. After you have exhaled, rest, release your hands, slowly lowering your arms out to the sides and downward. The palms turn down; lead with the heels of the palm. Let gravity pull your hands down, moving slowly, and then rest them lightly, palms up on your thighs. Smile into your liver, breathing deeply, and imagine you are still performing the liver sound. As with the lung and kidney sounds, do at least six repetitions.

The liver is associated with the gallbladder, the color green, the element wood, and because it is a generating, expanding energy, the season spring. Anger is the emotion traditionally associated with the liver. The positive emotion is kindness.

Heart Sound

This sound is performed in a relaxed sitting posture as with the lungs and liver sounds. Again, smile lightly into your heart as you relax. Take a few slow, deep breaths to focus your intent. When you feel as if you have made a good connection with your heart, slowly move your arms up and out to the sides, palms up. Breathe in deeply, slowly raising your arms over your head following this upward movement with your eyes. Interlace your fingers, and slowly turn your palms up toward the sky. As you are slightly leaning to the right, stretch your palms up and slowly over to the right in a light, easy stretch, gently pulling on your heart.

To make the heart sound, open your mouth, as you round your lips and exhale slowly while making a *HAWWWWW* sound. Visualize your heart releasing heat, impatience, arrogance, hastiness, and cruelty. Focus on your heart and visualize the color red filling your heart as you softly smile into the area. Let your heart be soft and at ease. Practice this sound at least six times. The use of this sound can assist in the treatment of various ailments, such as sore throats, cold sores, swollen gums or tongue, heart disease, skittish behavior, and moodiness. The heart is associated with the small intestine, the element is fire, the color is red, and the season is summer. It is a radiating energy. The negative emotions associated with the heart are impatience, hastiness, arrogance, and cruelty. The positive emotions are respect, love, joy, honor, and sincerity.

Spleen Sound

In a comfortable seated posture visualize your spleen and softly smile into the organ. Place your fingers just under your ribcage on the left side of your stomach. As you begin the WHOOOOO sound, softly press your fingers in, almost as if you were trying to massage your spleen. While making the sound, gently look up as you round the middle of your back outward. The spleen sound is deep, coming from the bottom of your abdomen. As you make the sound, feel the vibrations through your spleen and in your vocal cords. Let any worries or negative concerns fade and fill your mind with thoughts of fairness. Let your true, inner strength come alive.

After you have finished your exhale, smile into your spleen, stomach, and pancreas. Rest your hands lightly on your thighs, palms facing upward. While sitting in this position, breathe into this area and visualize the color yellow and a soft, light sensation of contentment and ease, letting all of your tension fade away.

Triple Warmer Sound

Chinese medicine divides the body into three energy centers. The upper center consists of the brain, heart, and lungs. This center is hot and radiates heat throughout the body. The middle center is warm and consists of the liver, stomach, kidneys, pancreas, and spleen. The lower center is cool and consists of the sexual organs, large and small intestines, and the bladder.

The *HEEEEEEE* sound is used to balance the temperature of these three areas. The intent of this sound is to bring the heat from the upper section down and the coolness of the lower section up. To perform this sound, lie on your back, feet about hip width apart, arms extended down at your sides and a relaxed distance away from your hips. Let your palms face upward (just like the yoga corpse pose). Now inhale deeply, filling up all three centers, and exhale the *HEEEEEE* sound subvocally. Visualize a soft wave of energy rolling down your body as you exhale, making the sound. Repeat this exercise at least six times. This is a great way to help you fall asleep as it is very relaxing. If you are feeling overwhelmed or overly stressed, this is also a good practice to help you settle down and return to your center.

Summary of the Six Healing Sounds

The six healing sounds can be practiced as a set by doing all six sounds together or one after the other. When performing them together, practice each one long enough to experience a deep feeling with the sound and movement before going on to the next sound. This will not take long to learn. Remember that these practices will continue to deepen and will bring you value if you practice them in a consistent, focused manner.

Abdominal Conditioning

This is a great reset to use for building power and strength. To avoid cramping, it's recommended to start these training exercises slowly. In case of any discomfort, it's important to stop immediately and take a few slow, relaxed breaths. Then begin again slowly but with less force. This practice conditions the body to perform for a longer duration and with more power. Use it to increase your endurance to your desired level. Do not, however, practice this exercise prior to a deep ritual meditation practice. It will build Yang energy in the mind right when you are attempting to settle down and become more Yin.

In and Out

Of all the abdominal conditioning drills, this one is the simplest. To aid gently and to help you become more aware of the motions, place your palm on your abdomen. To conduct this exercise, slowly pull your belly button in toward your spine, release it, and then pull it back out again while maintaining a slow, steady rhythm. As your strength grows, gradually increase the amount of gentle hand pressure you use to provide resistance and support the growth of your power.

Rolling Up and Out

To do this, roll your abdomen in toward your spine, move it up to your lower ribs, and then stretch it forward and downward while pushing out to the front in a wave-like manner. Use your hand to help direct the movement and increase awareness, much like in the previous exercise.

Rolling Up and In

This is performed by making a wave-like motion, rolling the abdomen up to the rib cage, in toward the spine, and back down again – the reverse of the Rolling Up and Out exercise. As with the Rolling Up and Out, practice using your hand to help guide the movement and build your awareness.

Circling Left and Right

In this motion, the abdominal muscles make a clockwise and

counterclockwise circle. The palms of your hands should be on your abdomen, circling your hands in one direction while keeping your abdomen still. As you develop coordination, this will aid in guiding the movement. You will soon gain control over each of your separate abdominal muscles with repetition, allowing you to isolate each movement slowly and accurately.

Engaging in abdominal conditioning exercises can be beneficial for increasing your energy levels and enhancing your ability to store the energy that you generate through your training. Practice abdominal conditioning daily. These are easy exercises to do at any time or anywhere. Do them as often as you like.

Moving Meditation Resets

Four Count Breathing

This Qigong breathing set can be performed in a number of different ways. Four count breathing is a great place to begin in order to develop an understanding of breathing patterns and connecting deeply with the breath. While this breathing set can be used as a great centering reset, it can also be used as a preparation for other ritual meditation practices or for strengthening and conditioning the body, when performed using the more aggressive variations of the set.

Four count breathing can be performed standing in a comfortable shoulder-width stance or sitting with good, erect alignment. Begin with your hands at your sides, then inhale deeply as you pull your hands up, palms upward, elbows at your sides. Use your breath to guide the movement until your hands reach your chest. Then turn your palms forward as you exhale, pushing your hands forward, keeping your hands chest high and about shoulder width until your arms are fully extended in front of you. As you exhale powerfully, make the *HAAAA* sound with your breath by lightly closing off your throat and contracting your abdomen. Now inhale, pulling the hands back to the chest. Exhale as you push downward back to the starting position, again making the *HAAA* sound and finishing with your hands beside your hips. Now circle your hands, and continuing the flow, inhale, and repeat the movement.

As you are practicing the set, on the inhales you will stand up slowly, only extending the legs to about 98 percent extension, never locking out the knees. And on the exhales, you will slowly sit down an inch or two, depending on your comfort. If your breath takes six seconds to move that inch or two, then that is fine. The rising and lowering of the legs will never pause, just as the breath will never pause. You will use this same coordination of breath and movement with the arms movements, never pausing, always following the breath.

As you do this practice, slow down and listen internally. Notice all of the subtle movements in the body. When you move your arms, you want to softly use every muscle in your entire body, smoothly connecting them as you glide through the movements. Developing this coordination where the physical movements of the body are in tune with the breath will help you develop deep levels of relaxation and awareness in the body.

Shaking

This is a great practice for bringing energy to the body and mind, increasing circulation, and building awareness and focus as you bring yourself into the present for enhanced performance or mental clarity.

To perform this practice, stand with your feet about shoulder width, knees softly bent, and with good posture. Then, as a preparation for the exercise, begin with three full, deep breaths. Take in as much air as possible without causing discomfort. Feel the chest and abdomen expand and stretch on the inhale and relax and sink on the exhale. To begin the shaking exercise, start with bouncing on the balls of the feet. The heels of your feet will only lightly touch the floor as you come down or may not touch the floor at all.

Find a good rhythm, almost as if you were jumping up and down on a pogo stick.

As you are bouncing, continue to breathe the same deep breath as you did during the preparation breaths, but now on the exhale make a soft, audible *HAAAA* sound. As you make the sound, scan through your body visualizing all of your tension shaking away. Start at your toes and feet, relaxing all of your muscles, feeling the vibrations of the movement and the sound in your bones. Then scan through the rest of your body: your calves, legs, hips, stomach, back, chest, shoulders, arms, hands, face, and scalp. Visualize the pores in your skin opening and softening. Let all of your organs feel a sense of release and ease.

This practice can be used for a quick two to three-minute reset, but it can also be used for longer periods for more conditioning and energetic stimulation. It is a great practice for experiencing the feeling of energy movement in the body. It is a good practice for beginners because they can feel the energetic experience immediately and this helps them feel more subtle energetic movements in other practices.

Cupping, Tapping, and Skull Thumping

This is a great practice for both stimulating energies and for bringing you to a present state of mind. It is also an effective tool for coming out of longer meditations as it actively brings circulation and awareness back into the body. There are many different Qigong forms that use cupping and tapping. For our purposes with regard to improving our yielding skills, we are going to use a very simple method that will give you great energetic results.

- **Tapping:** This is done with the fingernails. Curve your fingers, making a claw hand. Relax your wrists and shake your hand up and down so that your fingernails hit against the surface of your skin. The idea is to hit

firm enough to stimulate the bones underneath the skin you are tapping.
- **Cupping:** This involves making a cup shape with your hands, almost as if you were drinking water from your palms. As you bend your hands at the knuckles, squeeze your fingers together, and press your thumbs into the index finger, giving your hand a firm posture. When using this cupping position, you will strike the skin with your palms almost as if you were clapping your hands. When striking your body with your cupped hands, hit firm enough to feel a light sting on your skin. This will make your skin warm and even turn it slightly red.
- **Skull Thumping:** This uses your hands and fingers to lightly tap and put pressure on various parts of your skull.

We will begin by using our tapping claw hands and tapping the feet, both on the top and the bottom of the feet, hitting firm enough to stimulate the bones of the foot. Then move up the shin tapping the shinbone up and down the shin about three times.

Next, use your cupped hands and follow the same pattern, hitting the feet, moving up the shin, and continuing all the way up the thigh on the front and back of the leg. Continue using your cupped hands to strike your skin around your hips. As you move up your leg, only move up about one inch at a time, hitting at least two to three times in each location.

Follow this by holding your left arm out straight in front of you at about shoulder height. With your right cupping hand, begin at the left hip and strike up the left side of your torso, slowly moving up about one inch at a time, all the way up to the upper lat area (latissimus dorsi muscle). Then the right hand starts at the fingertips of the left hand, which you are still holding out straight in front of you at shoulder height. Striking up the hand and moving up the arm, move slowly all the way to your shoulder and the base of your neck. Continue to cup this area as you lower your arm so that you release any tension that may be there from holding your arm out. Repeat on the other side.

The next act is to slightly bend forward and, using your cupping hands, reach around to your back and cup over the kidneys. Continue to strike firmly, feeling a slight sting with each strike. Strike this area for at least thirty to ninety seconds. Then, to move into the skull tapping, use your claw hand position by bending your fingers, making the shape of a claw, just like you would if you were scratching your leg. Begin by tapping on the center of your head at your hairline, on the top of your forehead. Start with both hands at the top and move slowly from the top center of the head down to just above the left and right ears. Then move your hands back up to the top but a couple of inches back on your head, tapping your way down to just above the backs of your ears. Repeat this pattern two to three more times, working your way around your head until you reach the back of your neck.

Begin skull thumping by placing your palms over your ears with your middle, ring, and pinky fingers pressing firmly into and around the back of your head. Using the index fingers, press into the top of your middle fingers. Build a resistance, then release, letting the index fingers thump the back of your skull. Your palms should be pressing in over your ears and as you are thumping the back of your head, you will hear an echo from covering your ears. As you are doing this, open your mouth and lightly tap your teeth by opening and closing your jaw. Do about eighteen to thirty-six repetitions.

Next, in this order, tap each area six to twelve times. Start by tapping above your eyebrows, just firmly enough to send vibrations into the skull. Then, tap below your eyes followed by tapping on your upper lip. Next, move to your jaw and tap again there. Finally, move the tapping to your chest and tap the center of your chest with both hands firmly for at least thirty seconds. Then relax with your hands resting at your sides.

Close your eyes for a minute in this position and notice any subtle energetic or physical changes you are feeling. This exercise is wonderful for stimulating your energy and bringing you to the present moment.

Mental and Philosophical Meditation Resets

Mental and philosophical resets are great for helping spark your creativity, reprogram your mind, and expand your intuition.

Gratitude Meditation

This meditation gives you a sense of happiness and is a great vibrational place to spend time. You can do this anywhere at any time; it is a good, positive mental exercise. When you pay homage to the universe and are happy to be standing in the place you are in, it gives you a sense of peace and ease. To magnify this practice, feel your gratitude expand and give thanks for everything in your life that merits appreciation. For example: having access to food and clothing, having a roof over your head, for the good people who you have been fortunate to spend time with, for some of the amazing places you have traveled, or for experiences you have been through, and most importantly, for the miracle of existence, your life, the gift that was given to you in order for you to be here listening, or reading, about this program.

The more often you feel gratitude toward these things in your life, the more often you will attract these types of experiences, people or good times to be enjoyed in your life. This is a great practice and it is easy to do. You can sit in silence and reflect at a deeper level, or you can practice this as you are walking down the street on your way to lunch. Use it as often as you can.

Affirmation Resets

These help develop a focused, positive mind. Affirmations are powerful tools that will help you achieve higher levels of success with your meditation practice, personality adjustments, motivation levels, or anything else that you are trying to accomplish. Our thoughts lead to our actions, our actions help us develop habits, and our habits reflect our personality. Our personality traits represent who we are. If there is something about who you are that you want to change, the best way to initiate that change is to control the thoughts that enter your mind. For example, you could choose the quality that you want to develop. It could be consideration, forgiveness, patience, health, compassion, creativity, or love. It is important to find something that is valuable to you, possibly even something that creates an emotional response. The practice is easy once you have decided on a quality that is important to you.

For this example, we will use consideration. The next step is to say to yourself "I am considerate." Repeat, "I am considerate" for at least two to three minutes. If you are in a place where you can comfortably say this audibly, all the better, but it can also be repeated internally. Focus on the word and how it makes you feel to experience this quality. You will soon find that this quality becomes part of who you are. Continue to use this practice and focus on one word for at least three to four weeks. Repeat this drill at least three to six times every day. You will find that after only a short while you will become more considerate.

Qigong's Four Hs

The 4 Hs of Qigong are Health, Humility, Happiness, and Harmony. This is a simple practice that helps bring a sense of ease to your heart. These four important virtues are cultivated when developing a meditation practice. This is a simple meditation you can use to bring your attention and thoughts to these 4 Hs and experience the feeling of having these powerful words influencing your life. The first step is to focus on your heart. Bring your attention to the center of your chest and feel a warm, relaxing energy there. Visualize letting go of any tension in your body. Then, focus your attention on your heart and imagine your breath flowing in and out of your heart and chest area.

Next, think about Happiness. Think of something that makes you smile, recall a positive feeling or a time when you felt happy inside. Then try to reexperience that place and time in your awareness. Continue to reflect on this feeling and enjoy the space that comes with this focus.

Once you are in this relaxed, peaceful place, reflect on your Health and how you are making positive choices to live a healthier lifestyle. Then think about how to maintain a confident sense of humility, to always be respectful to everyone you meet. Lastly, focus on being Harmonious and finding the rhythm that helps to keep you happy, humble, healthy, and at peace with yourself.

You can do this reset for a few minutes or it can be used as a longer meditation as well. You can pick either one or all of these words to focus on. The most important thing to remember is that in order to experience the most from this exercise, you must take the time to truly experience the feeling that comes when your attention is focusing on these words.

Summary – How to Use Meditation Resets

The most important thing to remember when you begin using resets is to develop the habit of using them throughout your day. You may want to start with just one or two of these resets. Make sure you have a system to help keep you consistent while you are forming these new healthy habits. You could keep a journal or set reminders on your phone or computer. As you practice these resets, notice which resets are energizing, calming, or even just catch your attention. Being in tune with these sensations gives you the ability to identify the best resets you need to balance any physical or emotional distractions. Remember, resets are brief. They are not intended to take you away from the things you need to do.

10

TAPPING INTO QI AND JIN

This chapter begins by explaining some of the underlying principles that govern the creation, movement, and nurture of Qi. Meditation's goal is the increase of both the Qi and Jin energies within the body and learn how to control and direct the movement of Qi. Jin energy is both external and internal. External Jin is purely muscular strength. Internal Jin is the internal Qi's build-up and circulation and is a Yin manifestation of energy. Whenever you use Jin, it must be supported by Qi. Jin and Qi should never be separated. At this point, if you are convinced that yielding is a skill set that you want to improve, this chapter offers some fundamental ideas and practices that will help you fine-tune your ability.

Your conscious mind must learn to lead your Qi. An ancient Chinese story illustrates this point: A Chinese emperor had a large pearl that he wanted to put on a string. Nonetheless, the pearl's perforation was not a straight line; instead, it had nine curves. It was impossible to push the string through it. A wise man tied a delicate thread to an ant and guided the ant to walk through the nine-curved channel while pulling the thread.

In the same fashion, your mind must learn how to lead the Qi throughout your body from the skin to deep inside the bones until it reaches every last part.

By cultivating your Qi, you can develop the internal energy called Jin, which will be far superior to external Jin, which is purely muscular strength. This coordination will give you more physical power and enhance your mental clarity.

Discussion of the various Qi-building meditation practices forms the bulk of this and the following chapter. This chapter focuses on meditations related to Breathing and the Small and Grand Circulation approaches. Remember, as you are building your practice, the best approach is to start slow and remain consistent. You will experience good results with only a beginning commitment to perform one ritual practice for fifteen to twenty minutes per day and to do a physical or philosophical reset every ninety minutes. Before moving into the discussion of the specifics related to the breathing and circulation meditations I will layout principles that should underlay all of your ritual meditation practices.

Tai Chi Chuan's Five Point Mind Approach

When developing a ritual practice, it is important to understand what your goals are and how the different meditation practices will influence your body, mind, and emotions. Tai Chi Chuan (sometimes called "Taijiquan") promotes a five-point conscious mind approach to understanding the basic principles behind any meditation practice.

1. **The balance of Yin and Yang governs:** Yang represents the body and its movements. Yin is the foundation of spirit, intent or direction, and energy or Qi. This mind approach presents a mutual reinforcement of Yin and Yang, which leads to harmony both internally and externally. There are Yin and Yang energies in everything. In our bodies, we experience these energies

physically, mentally, and emotionally. Externally we see these energies in our relationships, work, and our environment. By increasing your awareness through meditation, you will be able to see clearly when you are deficient in a particular area or need to change your balance of energy, either internally or in external situations.

2. **Intent guides everything:** Your intent guides every practice with breath, movement, and thought. The intent is powerful enough to help you build positive momentum and overcome blockages.

3. **Your heart should guide your intent to lead your Qi:** Your intent leads your Qi to achieve your desired outcome. For your intent to become a desired action, you must subconsciously use your heart to initiate that action. This is the Yin and more powerful side of the equation.

4. **The body follows intent and Qi:** Your intent and Qi are like the leaders in charge, with the body following their direction. This is easy to experience with simple tasks such as grabbing a glass of water where you form the intent, and your body gathers and aligns its energy to take the desired action. The magic lies in developing a subtle awareness of your intent and your Qi as it occurs and before the physical body responds.

5. **Focus on intent first:** This allows you to change the habit of resistance, eliminate stiffness, and build physical and mental flexibility. This process is the root of the meditation practice you are building. The more you understand the subtle details of this process, the deeper your meditation practice will become.

Mastering the Breath

Fundamental to building and moving Qi is the act of breathing. Mastering your breath is essential to developing a deep, profound internal art or meditation practice. You can use your breath to control your energy, mood, focus, intent, and power. Using your breath as a strategy to balance your life will enable you to act more harmoniously in everything you do. With all of the outside distractions in today's society, it is easier than ever to lose track of your breath. Emotional disturbances, changing routines, outside demands, and internal conflicts can all cause changes in your breathing, disrupting your natural flow. Poor breathing habits often lead to high blood pressure, increased stress, panic attacks, lack of focus, and high levels of tension, as well as other health problems. Developing a strong foundation with your breath is essential if you want to have a deep meditation practice and maintain a healthy lifestyle.

Many of us constantly hold our breath throughout the day. This often causes tension and mental distractibility. As soon as you begin to hold your breath, you begin to tense up, losing your natural, relaxed state. Some meditations use breath-holding exercises to build tension. This chapter, however, teaches how to build a consistent, smooth breathing rhythm with your breath. Once you have learned the basic breathing exercises and have developed a relaxed, baseline breathing rhythm, the next step is learning how to strengthen your breath and build power and energy. When first learning the exercises that follow, it is best to perform them in a comfortable sitting position with your spine upright and relaxed.

Chest Breathing

This is a simple exercise you can do anywhere. You can use it as a still meditation or practice it as you are walking or going about your daily activities. First, visualize your lungs. Then take in a full inhale and expand your lungs, focusing on all sides: front, back, left, right, bottom, and top. Let your upper body be relaxed and continue to breathe deeply.

While performing this breath, take in as much air as you can comfortably while staying soft and relaxed. If you are being too aggressive with your breath, you may experience cramping and defeat the goal of becoming calm and relaxed. After practicing this breath for two to four months daily, it will become natural and you will eventually find yourself doing this breath unconsciously, without monitoring. This is your ultimate goal. Once you have reached this point, you can continue with this strategy for as long as you like. There are endless benefits that come with developing this practice. Or you can move to the next breathing practice in this series.

Normal Abdominal Breathing

This exercise also uses your maximum lung capacity. Over time, as with any of these breathing strategies, you will find your lung capacity expanding. You will be able to take longer, deeper, more relaxed breaths. With this strategy, you will bring your focus to your abdomen and your lower torso. When you inhale your abdomen, your sides, and your lower back all expand. Your perineum will open or expand softly downward. On the exhale, these areas will all lightly contract. This is a very relaxed breathing method. It is often used by many different meditation practices.

While this method is relaxing, it also delivers naturally balanced breathing. The inhale breath is Yin in nature. The exhale breath is Yang in nature. This balanced breathing allows for harmony and ease of mind, giving the practitioner the ability to have deep, relaxing meditations. As your practice becomes smooth and natural, you will find yourself subconsciously using this abdominal breathing. You can then move on to the next breathing strategy.

Reverse Abdominal Breathing

This is the first active breathing strategy for leading the energy or Qi within the body. On the inhale breath, the abdomen, lower torso, and the perineum all contract softly. These actions are all Yin in nature. Then on the exhale breath they all expand and become Yang in nature. Once all areas involved in breathing are either Yin or Yang, it will be easier to direct your Qi toward your desired outcome.

Some say that reverse abdominal breathing is not natural and may be dangerous. This is not true at all. If you think about how your breath works, you will see that you use this breath every day. Your body will naturally use reverse abdominal breathing when you need to generate more power. For example, when you are about to push or pick up something heavy, you naturally use reverse abdominal breathing. It may not be a conscious decision, but your body uses this breath to generate more power and strength.

This type of breathing generates more power because as you exhale you use the Yang side of your breath. This means you are sending a charge of Qi energy through the nerves in your body, giving your muscles maximum power. Another instance when your body will naturally switch to this type of breathing is when you have an emotional response that results in laughing or crying.

When you practice reverse abdominal breathing as a meditation, you want the movements to be relaxed and soft. If you try to generate too much power, you may get cramping, just like when you have laughed or cried so hard that your belly hurts. This results from performing the reverse breathing with too much force. While meditating, relax and use slow, deep breaths with soft abdominal movements. As you become accustomed to this breathing strategy, you will be able to increase the volume of the breath while maintaining a relaxed state. Once you are able to do this, you can move to the next breathing strategy.

Embryonic Breathing

By the time you reach the stage to begin using embryonic breathing, you should have been practicing breath work for at least three to six months and be able to easily maintain a comfortable, smooth breath throughout most of the day. You can do any type of breathing exercise once you master the embryonic breathing method. You will be using the reverse embryonic abdominal breathing and performing this strategy with the intent to lead the energy to the center of your lower dan tien. The lower dan tien is often referred to as your second brain. It is located in the center of your lower abdomen. This area is used to store energy, in a sense, similar to a battery.

The first step when practicing embryonic breathing is to focus on the center of your brain, which is called the "upper dan tien." This is the same location as the pineal and pituitary glands. To locate this point, visualize a line going through your head from the front top of one ear to the front top of the other ear. Also, visualize another line following the bottom of the valley between the left and right hemispheres of your brain. This line will be, approximately, from the center of the eyebrows to the center of the back of the head. Where these two lines cross will be the center of your head. Another trick you can use to find this center is to make the *HMMMM* sound. This will vibrate in the center of your brain, and you will be able to feel the center of the upper dan tien.

Bringing your focus to this area will help quiet your mind. This is one of the most difficult tasks when doing any meditation. When you are sleeping, your consciousness naturally resides in this area, creating a stronger connection with your subconscious mind. By focusing on this area, it will be easier to tap into the subconscious mind while awake. It will also help you experience more profound meditations. Taoists often refer to this area as the "mud pill palace." It is said that if you can bring your energy down to this level, the seed (or mud pill) that resides in the center of the mud will sprout up out of the mud and allow you to see life more clearly.

Once you understand where to direct your focus, the next step is to use your inhale breath to bring your energy inward to this location. This will calm down your brain activity and your mind will become clear. If you keep your awareness in this location, you will be focused and at peace. After you are able to bring your focus and energy to the center of your brain, the next step is to lead your Qi to the center of your lower dan tien. The lower dan tien is located by drawing a line starting three inches below your navel, traveling through to your L3 vertebra in your spine. The next line is from the top of your left hipbone to the top of your right hipbone. These two lines cross at your center or lower dan tien.

On the inhale breath, bring your energy inward, and on the exhale breath to relax, as you keep your intent on your center. The upper and lower dan tiens are connected by the spinal cord. The fluid in your spinal cord consists of material that is highly conductive of bioelectric energy. The communication between your upper dan tien and lower dan tien is virtually immediate; therefore if you are breathing into the center of your lower dan tien, you will also be in the center of the upper dan tien. However, you will never be able to achieve focus on the center of your lower dan tien if you cannot find and maintain the center of your upper dan tien.

The embryonic breathing strategy is good to have as part of your daily ritual. It is a core meditation that you should try to perfect if your desire is to become a devoted meditation practitioner. The goal is to gain the ability to focus on the center of the lower dan tien. If you find yourself thinking about the upper and lower dan tiens simultaneously, this is called two polarities breathing, not embryonic breathing. Once you have the ability to calm your mind and embryonic breathing becomes natural, you can move on to other breathing strategies. However, the goal is not to memorize as many breathing strategies as possible – it is to become proficient in the ones you know.

It is important to experience the many benefits each breathing method offers. This only happens if you reach deep levels with each and truly experience the feeling associated with each of them.

I recommend doing the embryonic breathing for at least six to twelve months before you move on to the Small or Grand Circulations. Embryonic breathing should be a skill that you never stop practicing. Do not look at embryonic breathing as a stepping stone to more advanced practices because this is one you need to master and use for the rest of your life.

Small and Grand Circulation Meditations

The purpose of the Small and Grand Circulation meditations is to lead Qi energy to specific locations. Both are used in healing practices. The Grand Circulation is also used for power in martial arts. The Small Circulation meditation works by leading Qi energy through various vessels in the body. Its focus is on basic healthful circulation. It is good to be at a competent level first, before undertaking the Grand Circulation meditations. The Grand Circulation is also about circulating the Qi energy. It, however, hones the practitioner's intent, allowing that enhanced intent to direct the energy to a specific location for martial arts or healing.

This discussion of Small and Grand Circulation meditations relies on Chinese medical terms. Chinese medicine, with its emphasis on the body's energy processes, has mapped and named key energy functions and points throughout the body. Western medical practice traditionally has a different approach but that is changing as more Western doctors incorporate Chinese approaches, such as acupuncture, into their treatment protocols. Some of the Chinese medicine terms used in the discussion below may be unfamiliar. To begin, it is helpful to visualize the purpose and pathways of the three primary vessels used by both methods the: governing, conception, and thrusting vessels:

- **Governing Vessel:** This travels up the spine starting at the hui yin, or perineum, and continues around the head to the roof of the mouth. The governing vessel is the point where all the Yang channels converge. For this

reason, it is said to govern all of the body's Yang channels. The point is known as the "Sea of Yang Meridians" or "fire vessel" because it controls all the Yang channels in the body, and stimulation of this point can help increase Yang energy. Its pathway runs along the spine, which is a Yang area of the body.
- **Conception Vessel:** The conception vessel, also known as the "Sea of Yin" or "water vessel," plays a significant role in Qi circulation by monitoring and directing all of the Yin channels. Unlike the Governing Meridian, which runs along the midline of the back from the perineum to the roof of the mouth, the conception vessel runs up the front of the body, from the perineum to the tip of the tongue, forming a circular pathway in conjunction with the governing vessel.
- **Thrusting Vessels:** A key function of the Thrusting vessels is to establish a connection, facilitate communication, and provide mutual support between the conception and governing vessels.

Discussion of the Grand Circulation meditations also mentions the other Chinese medical terms, some of which were touched on previously and others that are new. These are briefly described in the following list as well as again in the paragraphs in which they appear.

- **Baihui Point:** The Baihui Point, located on the highest point of the head and is an important point on the governing vessel, it is commonly used in neurology and psychiatry as well as a distal point of anorectal disorders by acupuncture practitioners. It is known for its therapeutic effects in relieving headache, stroke, dizziness, and anxiety.
- **Daz Hui Point:** This is the point situated in the center between your shoulder blades.

- **Hui-Yin Point:** Hui-Yin Point, also known as the "Meeting of Yin Point," is located in the perineum region, which is the area between the anus and genitals. It is an important acupuncture point that is associated with the kidneys, bladder, and reproductive system.
- **Loa Gong:** These points are located in the center of your palms. They extend past your hands six to twelve inches.
- **Lower Dan Tien:** This is often referred to as your second brain. It is located in the center of your lower abdomen. If you were to draw a line from three inches below your navel to L3 vertebra and another from the top of one hip bone to the other, where they cross would be the center of the lower dan tien.
- **Ming-Men Point:** This is sometimes called the "Gate of Life." This point is located along the spine below the kidneys and is the point where the energy from the lower dan tien meets the energy flowing from the upper dan tien.
- **Upper Dan Tien:** This is found in the center of the brain, in the same location as the pineal and pituitary glands.

The Small Circulation Meditation

This meditation helps balance and build the energy throughout the body by having a smooth circulation in the conception and governing vessels, allowing you to naturally supply energy to the twelve energetic channels in the body. The governing vessel travels up the spine starting at the hui yin, or perineum, and continues around the head to the roof of the mouth. The conception vessel is located on the front side of the body and runs from the hui yin point (perineum) up to the tip of the tongue.

When practicing the small circulation, you will use reverse breathing as we did in the embryonic breathing. It will help you lead the Qi up the governing, fire vessel and down the conception, water vessel. This is a great practice for balancing the body's energy. If the conception (water vessel) and the governing (fire vessel) are free of blockages, it will be easier to open all the other vessels in the body and to make the entire energetic body function more smoothly.

As with the previous exercises, begin this practice in a comfortable sitting position. Start with a few reverse abdominal breaths to relax. Begin to focus and let go of any outside distractions. The tip of your tongue will lightly touch the roof of your mouth, making a closed circuit for the energy to travel around the outside of your torso and head, connecting the conception and governing vessels. To find the correct place for your tongue, move the tip of your tongue around on the top of your mouth. The place that is most sensitive, usually about one to two inches behind your top front teeth will be the spot. To begin the circulation, on the inhale visualize a soft wave of energy moving up your spine from your lower dan tien, past the perineum, and all the way up to your neck. Lead the Qi around the center of your head to the roof of your mouth. From here, start your exhale, leading the Qi from the tip of your tongue down the conception vessel and back to your lower dan tien.

To increase your intent and the power of the circulation, as you inhale and the wave of energy passes through your ming-men point (sometimes referred to as "the gate of life"), which is located along the spine below the kidneys, visualize energy flowing and joining with energy from your lower dan tien, like two rivers joining forces to increase the flow. As the energy is flowing up your spine, each vertebra should be relaxed and open, lengthening to allow for the best circulation. Your breath should be soft, smooth, and long. If you have taken the time to be proficient with embryonic breathing, it will not take long for you to feel the energy flowing around this path. With practice, you will feel the flow become very strong.

Remember that it is your intent that must lead the energy on this path. If your intent gets stuck or falls behind the circulation, it will lose power. Your intent needs to lead the energy, always staying slightly ahead of the energy flowing through the conception and governing vessels. Practicing your spinal rotations from the reset section will help you to gain awareness along your spine and allow you to advance your small circulation practice at a faster pace.

The Grand Circulation Meditations

These four meditations are often used with movement as well as still meditations. They have many health and physical benefits. Grand Circulation is a common practice in martial art applications, but it is also helpful for athletes in any sport to fine-tune their practice and learn how to generate more power in their movements. This breathing strategy is similar to the small circulation breathing strategy. Grand Circulation practice begins the same way with the energy flowing up the spine on the inhale, but only until it reaches the daz hui point, which is located between your shoulder blades, along your spine. Then on the exhale, the energy travels horizontally from the daz hui point, across your shoulder blades, through your shoulders, down your arms, and out of your hands through the loa gong points. These points are located in the center of your palms or your fingertips.

There are numerous ways to practice the Grand Circulation. The reason these four particular exercises are included in this chapter is that they are simple and will help you to lay a solid foundation for your practice. With these breathing strategies, you will quickly feel a good energy flow, especially if you have become proficient in the previous strategies.

Primary Rolling

This is the first practice in the Grand Circulation set. Stand in a shoulder-width stance with your knees slightly bent. The outsides of your feet should be parallel. Lengthen your spine from your tailbone to the crown of your head, standing upright with arms relaxed at your sides. Begin the breath, making a soft wave-like movement as the energy moves, softly rolling up your spine. When the energy reaches the daz hui point in the center of your shoulder blades, let the wave continue across your shoulder blades, rolling down your arms and extending down and out through your hands as you exhale. It may take a little practice to coordinate these subtle movements, but it will come quickly if you are smooth and relaxed, and you let the movement naturally flow with the circulation.

This primary rolling can be used as a basic beginning to all Grand Circulation exercises. It is also good for the health and the physical side of training. Remember not to focus on where you feel the energy. Instead, stay slightly ahead of it, with your intent leading the energy and allowing it to gain momentum and power. When you reach your hands with the circulation, visualize the energy flowing out of either the loa gong point or your fingertips and extending past your hands at least six to twelve inches.

The next four sitting Grand Circulation Practices are great for enhancing your overall awareness of the energetic movement in your body. They can also help you to reach deep profound levels of meditation. These are used for enhancing health, spiritual enlightenment training, increasing focus, and developing power.

During these practices it is important to maintain a comfortable sitting posture so that you are not distracted by discomfort or lack of balance. You can use a chair with your back straight and your feet parallel, relaxed on the ground. If you need back support, you can find some pillows or cushions to help with comfort. If you do use some sort of back support, make sure not to lean into it. You want your spine to be free; allow it to move with your breath.

If sitting on the floor with a cushion or mat is comfortable for you, that is fine. It is recommended to sit with one leg slightly in front of the other to avoid cutting off circulation by crossing your legs. Remember, you need to feel comfortable in order to reach deep levels of meditation. If you are new to the practice, play around with a few different sitting methods and see what works best for you.

Grand Circulation Meditation

This sitting exercise is excellent for health and focus. Sit in a comfortable sitting posture. Place one palm over your lower abdomen and your other palm over the first. Begin the breathing and inhale using the reverse abdominal breathing strategy. Lead the energy up your spine to the daz hui point feeling that soft wave moving with a light momentum up your spine. Exhale and release across your shoulder blades. Let the energy flow away from your spine, through your shoulders, and down your arms. As it reaches the loa gong points in the center of your palms, inhale and bring the Qi back into the circulation through the abdomen for another cycle. You can do this for as long as you like. Spend some time with this and become familiar with the subtle communication your breath is having with your body. The more in tune you become with these subtleties, the stronger your energy will become.

Grand Cleansing Circulation Meditation

This meditation is a sitting practice good for releasing stress, lowering blood pressure, and calming the mind. To begin this practice, sit in your comfortable sitting posture. To begin the grand cleansing breath, find the center of your lower dan tien (see Embryonic Breathing instructions if you do not recall how to do this). Inhale to your lower dan tien using the reverse abdominal breath. Now exhale, releasing the energy down and out through your perineum. As the energy flows out of your perineum, it circles up the outside of your body, moving up towards your head. Then start your inhale, continuing the upward flow of energy around and into your bai hui (the center, top of your head) and then down to your lower dan tien to complete the cycle.

Visualize this energy coming in through your head, traveling down the center of your spine to your lower dan tien. You can do this for three to six minutes as a starting point for other practices, or you can practice it for as long as you like if you feel the need to unwind or release. If you are practicing meditations and you feel the energy is getting too strong or uncomfortable, use this strategy to bring it back down and find a comfortable balance before continuing.

Grand Storing Circulation Meditation

This sitting practice will help you accumulate the energy for healing meditations, building your immune system, and strengthen your energy. It is also used for more advanced meditations like Nourishing Grand Circulation, which is discussed in the next section. To begin this version of Grand Circulation, start by sitting in your comfortable sitting posture. On your inhale, visualize taking in all of the positive energy around you and bringing it into your ba hui point as in the grand cleansing strategy. Then, focusing on the inhale breath, bring the energy to the center of your lower dan tien. When you exhale, keep your intent on the center of your lower dan tien and visualize your energy building. Do not release the energy outward as in the grand cleansing strategy. This storing circulation can be done as often as you like. If you feel the energy getting too strong and uncomfortable, just start doing the cleansing breath again to release some energy.

Nourishing Grand Circulation Meditation

This is another sitting meditation used for bringing energy to the upper dan tien for enlightenment and increasing your intuition. Our brain cells use twelve times the energy as most cells in the body, so in order for us to bring our mind to high levels of awareness, we need to supply the upper dan tien with more energy. To start, sit in your comfortable sitting posture. Again, find the center of your upper dan tien. As you inhale with your reverse abdominal breath, lead the energy up from your lower dan tien through the center channel (or spinal cord) to the upper dan tien. On your exhale, relax, but keep your focus at the center. Do not guide the energy outward. Repeat for as long as it is comfortable for you.

This is the training needed for the mind to have the power to open the third eye. Even if this is not your desire or you never reach this goal, you will find yourself becoming more intuitive, more aware of yourself, and more in tune with your surroundings by using this method.

The following chapter, Chapter 11, explores various aspects of the meditation practices of Standing, Tai Chi Chuan, and Qigong meditations – all of which are called "standing meditations." All of these build, direct, and nurture Qi.

11
STANDING AND MOVING MEDITATIONS

Standing Meditations

Standing meditation postures offer the most direct entrance to cultivating high levels of energy. Indian wall art establishes that this type of meditation has been used for over four thousand years. It has long been a fundamental component of most forms of Chinese martial arts. Every martial art incorporates these standing postures, or parts of these postures into its practice, making these meditations fundamental to every martial arts practice for all three elements of yielding: physical, mental, and emotional. Originally there were over two hundred standing postures forming the basis of all Chinese and Taoist martial arts. Today, there are many more.

Standing meditation opens energy channels in the body and reveals blockages in the body. This awareness allows the blockages to be addressed and the body to become healthier. Standing meditations will also help correct anybody's alignment problems. In the beginning, after only a few minutes of meditation, soreness or imbalances that need correcting will become readily apparent.

Once noted, one needs to adjust the posture in order to continue and maintain the meditation.

Standing meditations are used to build and store energy. Each meditation posture is related to different energetic channels in the body and is intended to bring out the innate power of the body, revealing the practitioner's latent abilities that were hidden before. Most of us have different understandings of relaxation. Some people have a difficult time letting go and being at peace in their minds. If the mind is not peaceful, the body cannot be rooted or relaxed. Standing meditations teach how to settle the mind. Once that is achieved, the communication between mind and body becomes smooth and light, even during times of both physical and emotional stress.

Good Posture and Alignment during Standing Meditations

Breath work is an essential part of your meditation training, but posture and alignment work together with the breath and are equally important. This section focuses on building a strong posture and enhancing your awareness of your alignment. Maintaining proper alignment will give you more energy because your body will not have to work as hard as it does when you are improperly aligned. When a weak posture is stressing your body, your thoughts will tend to be distressed and distracted. Whether you work at a desk job or perform physical labor, bad posture leads to problems. Initially, these problems may be subtle, but eventually, they can lead to illness and chronic health issues. As your postural awareness increases, the consistent use of the correct alignment in everything you do, from physical activities to sitting in a chair, will yield greater focus as well as improved mental and physical health.

Standing meditations are one of the best ways to develop a high level of postural awareness. Their purpose is to develop a strong root using proper alignment, relaxation, and increased flexibility. A strong root and proper alignment require flexibility, particularly in the body's lower half. Ankles, knees, hips, and the waist must move easily in order to maintain a solid root and central equilibrium. This flexibility enables you to adjust your position while remaining strongly rooted. Correct breathing is equally important when practicing standing meditation because it allows you to remain relaxed as well as to develop and maintain deep rootedness. Similarly, relaxation is also necessary because the tension in the body affects both breathing and the ability to stay firmly rooted.

In sum, if your body is out of alignment, it will work harder to maintain your posture. This will cause stress which will start to aggravate your mind and cause soreness. Once you have mastered correct alignment and built up your strength, you will be able to stand for a half-hour or longer. At that point, you will experience endless benefits from this practice.

Standing Meditation Preparation

When performing standing meditation, the goal is to use your skeleton to support your weight as much as possible, while your muscles remain active but relaxed, and your mind remains at ease.

To begin basic standing meditation, put your feet into a shoulder-width stance, keeping the outsides of your feet parallel and your knees slightly bent, as if you were about to sit down on a tall stool. Let your arms be relaxed at your sides with your middle fingers resting lightly on the outsides of your upper legs, or along the seams of your pants (a location called the "IT band").

Next, visualize opening the joints in your body, starting from your waist and moving down. Open your hips, knees, ankles, feet, and toe joints without increasing the height of your stance. You want to remain rooted. Open all the joints throughout your torso, softly tuck your pelvic bone, and lengthen each vertebra all the way up to the crown of your head. Open your armpits and your shoulders, as well as your elbows, wrists, and fingers. If you want to sit lower to build strength and increase your endurance, tuck your pelvis and release the muscles in your legs to lower your stance. Do not force this movement. Let it be natural.

Once you have established this opening of channels, the energy will begin to rise from your feet. Allow it to flow into your lower dan tien, where it will be stored. Do the same with your upper body, moving the energy down into your lower dan tien. You move the Qi energy by using your breath as a pump, sending the energy out from the lower dan tien on the inhale, opening all the joints and expanding, and bringing the energy back to the lower dan tien and storing it on the exhale. Continue this until your lower dan tien feels full and your energy flow strong.

Visualize the lower dan tien as functioning like a battery where energy is built up and stored. It stores high levels of energy that are useful for physical and mental health. Once you have learned how to store your energy, you will start to become healthier and stronger than ever before. It is possible to be healthy and not strong. It is also possible to be strong but not healthy. If you develop both health and strength, they will bolster each other, and both will grow stronger. Standing meditation develops strong healthy bodies and minds. As your practice grows, you will find that there is no limit to the amount of energy the lower dan tien can store.

Standing meditation may reveal limits on your physical abilities but, even so, its internal impact is limitless. No matter what the practice, always listen as closely as possible and notice all of the subtle clues your body and mind are presenting. Correct postural alignment can be very complex. Even the physical limitations may vanish or lessen as you practice if you learn to listen and let your mind communicate with your body. Standing meditation may seem simple, but that is if you are only looking at posture and remain unaware of how the meditation affects both the body and the mind.

The "Embrace the Tree" Standing Meditation

Once you have completed the preparation posture, you are now ready to move into the standing meditation postures. On your next exhale, release your hands away from your sides, letting them move involuntarily forward toward the fronts of your thighs. Inhale as your fingertips travel up your abdomen to your chest, and open to the number one posture. Your arms will be shoulder height in a circular shape as if you were hugging a large tree. This posture is sometimes called "Embrace the Tree," "Buddha at Post," or "Embracing Space." It can be practiced either in a narrow shoulder-width stance or in a deeper, wider stance. The outsides of your feet are parallel in the shoulder width stances. Toes should be slightly turned in. For the deeper, wider stances, your feet can be slightly turned out. In the narrower stance, your knees are slightly bent and not locked out. In the wider stance, you can sit low which will work on building more rootedness and strength.

Next, slightly tuck in your pelvis and slowly bow forward at your waist until you feel your weight lightly transfer toward the balls of your feet. Stop when you reach what is called the bubbling well, which is located just behind the balls of the feet. Keep your chest and shoulders relaxed. Your elbows should softly sink and energetically expand out to the sides with your relaxed breath and are slightly angled downward. The elbows can be slightly dropped for more physical power and slightly lifted if the focus is health.

The fingers are four to eight inches apart from the left hand to the right and softly spread apart, but not so much that they make your hands tight. Both middle fingers should point toward each other, pointer fingers lifting slightly towards the sky, ring and pinky fingers dropping toward the ground. Your thumb is lifting up as if it were hanging from a string.

Next, visualize a pencil traveling through your neck, starting in the soft space under the right ear and coming out under the left ear. Use this imaginary pencil as a pivot point to slightly lower your chin. After doing this a couple of times, notice how it allows the back of your neck to stay relaxed.

The next step is helpful for reaching deeper relaxation. Think back to the inner smile meditation you mastered several chapters ago, and visualize a light smile with the back of your throat. Let that smile continue down through your torso, bringing softness to your organs. This will immediately make you feel more rooted. Use this inner smile to help you to relax, achieve a stronger root, and settle the mind.

The inner smile is a great technique to practice all day long, whenever you think about it, until it becomes a natural habit. Not only will you find you are more focused, rooted, and relaxed, but your mood will also be consistently more positive. You will see a difference after only a short time. This is a powerful practice and well worth the time to make it your natural habit.

Your gaze should be horizontal and five degrees above the horizon, looking way off in the distance and staring into space. Do not stare at any one point. Let everything in your vision come in without focus. Do not project your intent outwards as if you were trying to see something. Just let whatever is in your field of vision come to you, watching lightly as it happens. This almost has the feeling of bringing your awareness to the backside of your body.

You can softly let your eyelids fall half closed or leave them open. Experiment with both methods and determine which one is more effective for your needs. To help with quieting your mind and increasing the depth of your practice, use a relaxed, soft breath that moves from your nose to the back of what some call the "third eye," located in your forehead between and above your two eyes. Feel the air slowly moving through your nose, down the back of your throat, filling your lungs and sinking Qi energy to your lower dan tien.

When your breath is natural and relaxed, your mind will closely follow. Deep and profound levels are reached once you have developed a smooth, consistent breathing rhythm during standing meditation. In the beginning, start with one or two five to fifteen-minute sessions a day. If you go for too long in the beginning, you may create problems because your alignment may not be correct. With consistent practice, you will be able to stand longer, until you reach the point where you can stand for as long as you like – even for hours at a time.

As you start to become more in tune with your alignment and root through your standing practice, the goal is to use this proper alignment throughout your day. When you can learn to move through the day while maintaining good posture, you will start to experience higher levels of energy, reduced physical and mental stress, and more harmony in your life.

Moving Meditations

Walking Meditation

Through the many different styles of walking meditations, you will find practices that help achieve different results. Integrating a walking practice into your daily flow can be extremely beneficial. Walking meditation is often used as a stand-alone practice but can also be used as a link to integrate your meditation into daily activities. This is increasingly valuable for guiding change and reaching new levels of awareness. As you grow consistent with your meditation practices, you will start to reach deeper levels of awareness and relaxation, becoming more in tune with your internal and external awareness. However, sometimes learning to integrate these practices into our daily activities is challenging. Walking meditation gives us a link to start moving through the day with awareness and helps to stay in tune with our heightened awareness we experience during meditations.

When we are working toward a change to become a better leader, athlete, businessperson, friend, spouse, parent, musician, or creator, we need a certain level of necessary, consistent attention to help things start to unfold toward our desired end goal. Walking meditation is a powerful tool to help bring your focused meditative mindset into your daily activities. This will often help us reach our goal of being a better "parent" because we are able to see the subtle cues to help us direct the daily situations towards a positive outcome.

The walking practice we are going to learn here is a simple one but very effective. Begin by standing with your feet side by side in a neutral position. Place your right hand in the center of your chest in a half prayer position and your left palm down by your left hip. Take a few slow relaxed breaths before you begin stepping. Every step is connected to the breath. On the inhale slowly peel your left foot up off the floor, as it is moving forward halfway through your step start your exhale then place the foot down softly. The heel of the stepping foot may not even clear the toes of the standing foot. It is not about moving fast or covering distance across the floor. Feel the breath and let the movement follow the breath. As you practice this method ten to fifteen minutes a day for the next two to three months, you will start to develop a deeper feeling of awareness through the movement. This is exactly what we are looking for to integrate the benefits of this practice into our day.

Tai Chi Practice

Most of us have seen in person, or on film, people practicing Tai Chi Chuan's slow, graceful movements. Tai Chi Chuan (sometimes called Tai Ji Quan, or Tai Qi Quan) is a moving, external meditation that creates internal tranquility. It is practiced worldwide because of its health benefits and its martial art applications. It is considered the fusion of the spiritual with the physical.

As we discussed earlier, Tai Chi's primary symbol, the Yin-Yang circle, is divided into two equal parts by a serpentine line which forms two fish-like figures curving into each other. One side is white, the other black, and each contains a small circle of contrasting color. The words, Tai Chi, translate as the "Grand Ultimate." The literal translation of the word, Chuan, is "fist." However, in Tai Chi Chuan, the word Chuan is a stand-in for the total physical body. Thus, the Chuan or body is the means by which the practitioner can experience Tai Chi – The Grand Ultimate.

Tai Chi practice is composed of sequential movements called "forms." The entire group of forms that compose a particular Tai Chi exercise is called a "set." A form is entered into slowly, the movement is performed, and then the form is slowly exited whereupon the practitioner slowly enters into the next form in the sequence. This progression is followed until the entire Tai Chi set is completed.

The nature of Tai Chi forms means that it is not possible to describe them with words. Most books describing the various forms rely on photographs, diagrams, or both. That is beyond the scope of this work. Moreover, there are a variety of different Tai Chi sets. The Northwest Fighting Arts Academy YouTube channel has some videos of a couple of the Tai Chi sets along with verbal explanations. You will also find detailed instructions on how to start a Tai Chi Practice at http://www.taichiandqigongonline.com/beginning. There are, however, important things to know if you want to take up the practice of Tai Chi.

Tai Chi has been evolving for more than seven hundred years and its composition is complex, making it difficult to pinpoint its exact components that constitute the art. Furthermore, art is always evolving from one generation to the next. For example, the current generation might specialize in the empty hand form and the sword whereas a prior generation was more focused on the fan and saber. Even teachers using the same set of forms can vary greatly in how and what they teach. Some masters may focus on the health benefits of the art while others could be more into the martial side of the training.

The Tai Chi concept is very adaptable and is applied in many different ways. Two people could learn the exact same form but train with different intentions to accomplish different outcomes. With the Tai Chi training, there are many areas such as sword, saber, short staff, long staff, fan, ball, spear, ruler, knife, various empty hand forms, warm-up routines, two-person sets, and pushing hands. The most common Tai Chi sequence is the Yang empty hand form. It has become increasingly popular due to the health benefits of the practice.

The emphasis on certain forms, principles, or training methods in Qigong may vary from teacher to teacher due to their individual experiences, temperament, or research in the practice. Most teachers will focus on only a few areas. There is a wide range and depth of understanding and knowledge available from the teachers. It is important to find a teacher that is best suited to your goals and who has the skills you admire.

In many cases, teachers will teach shorter, modified forms to increase the student's ease of learning the form. This modification makes it accessible to more people, but it also subtracts from some of the value taught through the original sequence. Those who are interested in a deep understanding of the art should learn all of the basic movements, long-form movements.

It is rare to find teachers who truly understand how to integrate coordinated breath and Qi (Chi) circulation into the form. Additionally, it is extremely rare to find a Tai Chi school well versed in the martial applications of the practice, the concept of Jin (the power generated internally and externally), two-person fighting sets, or Tai Chi pushing hands exercises. The reason for this is that many teachers and practitioners nowadays are seeking a convenient and efficient method for enhancing and preserving their well-being. Developing the other aspects of an art, such as technique, discipline, and creativity, through long and arduous training is a sacrifice that only a small number of individuals are willing to make.

In many cases, this is why some teachers, even when they are highly qualified, will hesitate to pass down the deeper aspects of the art to other than a few select students. There is concern that **these deeper aspects of Tai Chi Chuan, as well as those inherent in** Qigong training, may soon disappear from the art.

Whether or not a person learns Tai Chi depends on their attitude, consistency, and discipline. The first step is to make the leap and begin the training. It takes a strong will, perseverance, and patience to reach a deep level of understanding of Tai Chi Chuan. Moreover, the results are particular to each individual. Even two people with the same physical and mental abilities will find that their accomplishments differ. This difference will come from their manner of learning. The perfect student not only practices what they have learned but also reflects on it. The subsequent step is to conduct research and endeavor to attain a higher level of proficiency. Less strenuous learning will still yield benefits but, without an intense, focused learning approach, mastery of the art will remain unobtainable.

Tai Chi theory is deep and profound. It requires a significant amount of time to fully understand the intricacies of Tai Chi. This involves continuous learning, researching, reflecting, and practicing to reach a higher level of understanding and "enter the temple." However, the long-term benefits of Tai Chi are worth the effort, as even the smallest lesson learned can have a profound impact on one's practice for years to come.

There have been many times during my Tai Chi Chuan education when I learned a concept and understood at the time how to apply it. Then three, six, or even nine years down the road, I suddenly realized what the concept *really* meant.

This evolving way of learning is always exciting. It keeps you alert and present, eager to notice when the training yields something new. The funny thing about Tai Chi is that many times, the more you learn, the more you realize how much you do not understand. It is similar to a bottomless abyss or a flowing river that is both changeless and constantly changing.

Remember when taking up Tai Chi practice to find a competent teacher and then study wide and deep, investigate, contemplate carefully, discriminate between what is useful and what is not, and persevere in your practice.

Posture during Qigong and Tai Chi Chuan Sets

Many of the strategies we have been discussing such as breathing methods, some of the reset practices, and meditations come from Qigong. Like Tai Chi, there are many Qigong forms – more than you will ever want or need to know. There are too many to describe in this book. That said, I have found some of these forms to be very valuable and to be a fundamental asset to my development. Like many meditations, Qigong also has specific forms designed to help you achieve specific outcomes. Qigong forms focus on cleansing, lowering blood pressure, building strength, and increasing your Qi while helping with arthritis and a variety of other issues. If you would like to see what some of these different Qigong sets have to offer, you can check them out at https://portlandtaichiacademy.com/online-training/.

Whether you are practicing the Tai Chi Chuan forms, Qigong sets, yoga postures, or any movement meditation, there are some basic principles relating to posture that are important most of the time.

Head

In Qigong practice, the position of the head is crucial. It should feel as though it is suspended from above, as if there is a string attached to the crown of the head pulling it upward. This posture helps elevate the spirit of vitality and enables the body to move with lightness and agility.

In addition, the eyes should be focused with a concentrated spirit. When an individual has heightened and focused their spirit, their eyes will appear bright, and they will be able to perceive even the subtlest movements of their surroundings or opponent.

Torso

Another essential aspect of maintaining a central equilibrium in body awareness is to hold the chest in slightly, creating a slight sinking feeling. Arching the back between the shoulders creates a lifting sensation, allowing the chest to relax and the lungs to move naturally. This posture not only neutralizes an opponent's attack but also helps store energy within the body.

Additionally, the relaxation of the waist is a crucial factor in optimizing power and energy in Qigong practice. It serves as a fundamental link that allows for smoother, more flexible movements of the body. With a relaxed waist, practitioners can achieve better control over their movements, resulting in a more efficient use of energy. Maintaining proper alignment and relaxation throughout the body is essential to achieving the full benefits of Qigong practice.

Shoulders and Arms

To achieve better relaxation and facilitate the transmission of energy to the hands, it is recommended to sink the shoulders and drop the elbows. By maintaining relaxation and proper alignment in the body, the Jin energy can flow smoothly from the waist to the hands, allowing them to function as a unified and powerful unit. If the elbows and shoulders are not sunken, the Jin energy may become fractured and directionless. Moreover, sinking the elbows and shoulders can help seal major cavities such as the armpits against attack. Assuming a compact posture can enhance your ability to neutralize attacks as it allows for greater agility and ease of movement, making it easier to yield or re-deflect incoming attacks.

Hands

In martial arts, it is important to settle the wrists and extend the fingers. Settling the wrist involves dropping it slightly so that the base of the palm faces forward while extending the fingers helps promote efficient blood and Qi flow. When striking with the palm, the hand should be extended with the palm facing downward. Straightening the fingers and keeping them extended is important in martial arts as it allows for optimal efficiency in the flow of blood and Qi. This technique is crucial for developing greater accuracy and power in strikes. By holding the fingers straight, the energy can flow smoothly through the body and out into the strike, resulting in a more effective technique. Additionally, keeping the wrists settled and relaxed allows for more stability and control in the strike, further increasing its effectiveness.

Legs

Relaxing the thighs is a crucial aspect of body awareness in Qigong practice. The thighs are a crucial part of the body in generating force and movement as they serve to connect the waist to the knees. This connection allows for the smooth transmission of power from the lower body to the upper body. Proper use of the thighs can help improve balance, stability, and overall strength in martial arts and other physical practices. By keeping the waist and thighs relaxed and movable, you can improve the flow of Qi through the body and promote more efficient movement. The knees should be flexible like rubber bands, neither collapsed nor overstretched. They act as springs to release power and help maintain stability in the body.

Feet

Having a solid root is crucial for both martial arts and energetic practices, and it begins with the feet. To achieve a solid root, the feet should be firmly planted on the ground, providing a stable foundation for the body. When the foot is relaxed and connected to the floor, it is important to focus on the bubbling well point, which is located just behind the ball of each foot. This point is the center of gravity and helps maintain balance and stability. By paying attention to the bubbling well point, the body can move with ease and grace.

Breath

Coordinate the breath and the internal and external strength. Breathing, Qi (energy), muscular strength, and Yi (mind) must all act together. Your actions should be relaxed and coordinated with the breath. If breathing is tense, then there will be tension in the body and the mind will be distracted.

Whole Body Movement

The top and bottom follow each other with all body parts moving harmoniously together. During movement, there should be a sense of the body being connected such that the upper body and legs move together in unison.

Physical Awareness – Substantial and Insubstantial

Distinguish what is insubstantial and substantial. In traditional Chinese philosophy, the body is believed to have both aspects. A substantial aspect in the body refers to the physical form of the body, including the bones, muscles, and organs. The insubstantial aspect refers to the energy, or Qi, that flows through the body and animates it. This Qi is said to circulate through channels or meridians that connect the various parts of the body, and it is believed to be closely connected to the mind and emotions. In traditional Chinese medicine and martial arts, the balance and flow of Qi is considered crucial to maintaining health and vitality. A body or a body part is substantial when it feels strong, having pent up or releasing force – like being ready and then pushing a car. When insubstantial, the body or a body part, feels relaxed, though ready to intercept someone else's force and divert, deflect, or lead it in an advantageous direction.

In martial arts, it is common to have only one leg and one arm as "substantial" at a time, while the other leg and arm are "insubstantial." The determination of which part of the body is substantial or insubstantial in martial arts depends on the opponent's responses and the changes in their attacks. When the opponent is attacking with substantial force, the practitioner becomes insubstantial in that area to divert the force and avoid being overpowered. Meanwhile, the practitioner becomes substantial in another area, such as the opposite arm or leg or by shifting the entire body into a position from which they can effectively respond with force.

This concept is essential for maintaining balance, stability, and control during combat situations.

This type of awareness means it is important to know the manifestations of Yin and Yang in your own body. In martial arts, it is crucial to be able to discern whether an opponent's attack is substantial or insubstantial. Often an opponent will switch from asserting a substantial force to an insubstantial force and vice versa. This means also being aware of the opponent's Yin and Yang. In warfare terms, this type of awareness means, "I will know the enemy, but the enemy will not know me." This phrase often refers to the idea of "yielding to overcome." It means that while you are yielding or adapting to the opponent's movements, you are also controlling the situation and ultimately prevailing. This concept is often used in martial arts and can be applied to other areas of life as well. By being flexible and adaptable, you can gain control of a situation without becoming rigid or predictable.

In a negotiation scenario, this form of yielding can be applied effectively. For instance, let's consider a situation where you wish to modify your work schedule, but your supervisor is content with the current arrangement. To implement this strategy, you can address the objectives of your role, emphasizing their significance to you. Simultaneously, you can outline the potential benefits that align with these objectives, illustrating how adjusting the work hours would support and enhance them. By presenting a comprehensive case that highlights shared goals and potential positive outcomes, you can increase the likelihood of reaching a mutually beneficial agreement.

Mental Awareness

When you are in the middle of a technique, you should be 100 percent present and not splitting your attention. If you do, it will weaken your technique. When you use your mind to initiate movement, Qi is automatically circulated. In contrast, if you use your Li (strength), you will become tenser and Qi circulation will be hindered.

Qi energy in the body is in constant circulation, flowing down the front of the body toward the lower dan tien, where it is stored and then back up the spine to circulate throughout the body. This movement down the front of the body is considered Yin in nature, while the upward movement along the spine is Yang in nature.

Additionally, the mind plays a crucial role in directing the flow of Qi energy. Qi follows the mind, so where you focus your attention, Qi will accumulate. This is why mental and physical discipline is so important in Qi cultivation practices. When the breath, body, and mind are relaxed and working together, Qi can flow smoothly and harmoniously.

Using the Yi (mind) rather than the Li (strength) is also crucial in the practice of Qi cultivation and martial arts. By using skill, technique, and intelligence to defeat an opponent, rather than brute strength, one can reach higher levels of practice and overcome even more advanced practitioners.

Every movement from one to the next should flow smoothly with no force or opposition, the entire body remaining comfortable. In Tai Chi, each posture is part of a continuous, flowing sequence of movements. Each movement should be performed smoothly and with grace, so that the body is in a constant state of motion. This means that every part of the body should be engaged in the movement, either directly or by counterbalancing, to maintain balance and harmony throughout the sequence. The aim is to achieve a state of relaxation and ease while maintaining a strong and stable posture so that the energy (Qi) can flow freely through the body.

As the movements are performed the Yi (mind), Qi (energy), and body should be unified. Each posture should be neither too small nor too big and should feel comfortable and natural to the body. It is important that the body remains centered and upright, without any part hindering the flow of movement. This allows for a smooth and efficient flow of Qi energy throughout the body. The best results come from postures that are natural, centered, balanced, and controlled, with the arms neither too extended nor too drawn-in.

In order to attain a meditative state while moving through either Tai Chi or Qigong forms, you need to maintain stillness by keeping calm and your mind clear. Even when you are still, there should be a sense of the Qi energy dancing in your body. If, while in a meditative state, your Qi and body move naturally and correctly without conscious effort your movements will feel light, agile, flexible, and varied. This the underlying ideal of Tai Chi Chuan as a martial art first: the mind is cleared and the body relaxed, allowing the Qi to circulate.

By adhering to your opponent's movements and following their energy, you can maintain your balance and remain light on your feet, allowing you to respond quickly and effectively to any changes in the situation. This requires a high degree of sensitivity, relaxation, and skill, as you must be able to sense and respond to subtle shifts in your opponent's energy without losing your own balance or control. By cultivating this principle, you can become more agile, flexible, and adaptable in your movements, both in Tai Chi practice and in everyday life. If you attack and defend with a variety of techniques, you will be flexible. In this way, your intentions can be neither anticipated nor thwarted by your opponent.

While many of these strategies are related directly to martial training, the yielding awareness and understanding that comes with them can be applied to almost any area of life. If you start down this path, keep in mind there will be no overnight success stories. These skills take years to cultivate and reach high levels of understanding. I have been training many of these concepts for over thirty-five years and still consider myself a student. I frequently undergo further training with masters who I consider more advanced than myself. The key to developing a successful yielding capability, in all its many different facets and applications, is to approach the subject and the training with an open mind while learning to listen and learn with your entire being.

CONCLUSION

Three of the greatest challenges of my life were entering the Marine Corps and going to war, being willing to step into a boxing ring with someone who wanted to take my head off, and letting go of the walls of protection that were preventing me from being the person I know and respect today. The latter of the three challenges was the most difficult and a big part of the motivation behind this book.

Of course, I do not want to minimize either the horrific or the heart-wrenching aspects of war. While the war was challenging and life-changing, in many ways it was different. I had a good support system that helped me stay positive, and I was able to manage the stress in a way that helped me grow from the experience. The changes I went through during that time in my life were what put me on the path of martial arts, meditation, and the many philosophies behind these practices. As I began that journey, I experienced many transitions. With each transition I found myself experiencing them with growing confidence and certainty. The comparative ease of my latest progression through a transition is partially due to the fact that I am much older, more experienced, and capable of understanding these changes. Looking back, I can see how these life lessons gave me the motivation to dive into yielding training and to see the value in what it offers.

This book outlines many of the lessons I learned through my years of training. Some of them have become part of my daily ritual and some were used as building blocks to help build the foundation for my practice today. Yielding is something I practice and try to use in every area of my life. The training methods and philosophical ideas presented are tools you can use to reach depths of understanding in your personal development.

The book offers many commendable practices that deepen yielding skills. As you contemplate what and how to practice, the most important questions to ask yourself are, What practices will be fun? And, What practices will be inspiring? The answers will be unique to you because every individual is different. Fun and inspiration are important because the trick to reaching higher levels in your yielding skills is to be consistent, steady, and astute with your training.

Yielding practices employ logical progressions. But what distinguishes yielding training most of all, is the variety of practices it uses and the principles on which it depends. These deeply rooted principles are important because they are the bedrock on which each practice stands. The student who studies these principles and who consistently practices will assuredly experience profound physical and mental changes.

Make no mistake. Yielding is neither good nor evil. It can serve either of these motivations. However, those with an honorable character who are motivated to use their skills to serve the public good will always achieve more success at reaching higher levels of practice. By following your positive intentions and standing for principled choices, it is possible to enrich your character and discover a higher, more compassionate purpose within yourself – one that is worthy of commitment. This transformation will give greater meaning to your life and gift positive energy to everyone you encounter.

By now, you will have gathered that I believe human relationships are second only to survival in importance. You will recall an earlier chapter that discussed yielding in the context of relationships. I noted that if a conversation takes a negative turn, yielding skills can redirect the conversation back onto a positive track. I also noted that such a conversation needs to be redirected before it gains too much momentum in the wrong direction. This technique will leave you feeling better about the interaction and will allow all participants to move on to the next venture in a good frame of mind.

The physical aspects of yielding cannot be separated from yielding's impact on a person's thoughts and feelings. Because relationships are so important, their quality directly impacts any yielding practice. If you use yielding skills to show others that you value, care, and respect their well-being, you will find yourself reaching higher levels in your yielding practice. We all value the people who leave us feeling good about ourselves and life in general. Yielding practice teaches how to be one of those people.

I will always remember the feeling I was left with after training with one of my meditation teachers. Every Wednesday evening, a small group of us went to his meditation center and we listened to him talk about philosophy and then we practiced different meditations. The class lasted for three hours, and I always left feeling good and eagerly anticipating the next lesson. His ability to yield and to gift positive energy to people was like nothing I have ever experienced. One evening, after a particularly great session, he shook my hand. I felt his body vibrating through that handshake. His positive energy was so empowering that I felt like I just won the World Jiu-Jitsu Championship. I could not believe how intense and quickly my energy ramped up. It was an awe-inspiring experience that left me thinking how rewarding it would be if I could learn how to make people feel that good.

To earn a black belt in Brazilian Jiu-Jitsu is a tremendous accomplishment. After thirty-five years of practicing the martial arts, my educated guess would be that for every thousand people who start the practice of Jiu-Jitsu, maybe only two or three earn a black belt. And that is after nine to twelve years of seriously dedicated practice. This is a huge commitment.

Contrast this with the fact that, as a child, I received my first black belt in Chinese Kenpo after less than three years. Even if you are the smartest, best athlete on the planet, achieving a Jiu-Jitsu black belt in three years is next to impossible. So, there is a huge difference in the skill of a Black Belt who has taken twelve years to perfect his or her art versus someone who has reached that status in three years. Here I am making the point that, with meditative and martial arts, there will always be something more to learn. After thirty-six years of training in both, I still feel like I am as much of a student as I have ever been. These are arts that will always be impossible to truly "master."

It is only after we adopt yielding as a lifelong practice that we start to experience the benefits of the training. As time passes, the benefits and personal growth expand in ways that are unanticipated but welcome. I believe that yielding has made me a better martial artist, teacher, and person. A very important principle that I learned through my years of study is that developing these skills is an evolving process. The fundamental skills learned through studying the yielding arts have provided me and thousands of others, with the basis for a lifetime of growth.

Every one of life's rites of passage – high school graduation, college, and graduate school, earning a Jiu-Jitsu black belt, winning promotion at work, reaching a more profound understanding of life's meaning – are all new beginnings with new challenges and opportunities. Certainly, we need to learn from previous experiences to reach new levels in any endeavor. More importantly, however, we also need to discover when to let go of what we have learned. Only then will we be able to fully experience life and evolve in the here and now.

Long-term mediation and martial arts teach humility and appreciation for the unknown. These are attributes we need to use in every area of our life. It is okay to admit and accept that we cannot understand the why, how, and reason for everything that happens. Nor is it necessary to agree with everything and everyone we encounter. Still, being open, showing empathy, and learning from every opportunity that presents itself is what having a successful life is all about.

I believe that practicing the concept of yielding is essential to achieving a life of health, happiness, humility, and harmony. Do not consider yielding to be a bag of tricks, something to help you through your ups and downs. Instead, learn and nurture your yielding skills until they are firmly rooted in your character. To do so is to offer yourself the prospect of a life filled with the gratifying purpose and the deep joy that every human being deserves.

Yielding is an amazing concept. Hopefully, after reading this book, you understand why it is worth your time to apply these lessons to your life. If you do, I am very interested in hearing what lessons you may have learned through your cultivation of these practices. I will be grateful if you check out my Facebook page at https://www.facebook.com/TaichiYielding and let me hear about your thoughts and experiences related to yielding. Thank you.

The End

APPENDIX A: THE FIVE ELEMENT / PHASE THEORY AND YIELDING

As I said in a previous chapter, I was urged to study and apply the Five Element theory by every meditation and martial arts teacher I trained with over the past thirty-six years. Each declared that they used the theory to enhance their yielding awareness of themselves, others, and their environment. The five elements of the theory are Wood, Fire, Earth, Metal, and Water. Each teacher used the Five Element theory as a way to characterize the dynamics they found existing in every situation (the Dao or the Way).

There are three important things to know about the Five Element theory. First, it is more accurate to refer to it as the Five Element / Phase theory. This is because the term *element* suggests an unchanging state. Yet, the theory does not consider Wood, Fire, Earth, Metal, and Water to be unchanging elements of matter like atoms are in modern physics. Rather, the five elements are in a state of continual transformation, acting on each other and changing continually just like the seasons change from one to the next.

Secondly, the Five Element / Phase theory is especially applicable when one is evaluating the workings of the mind and spirit.

This is because it relies on the characteristics rather than the physical structure of the named elements.

Lastly, it is not possible to just flip a switch and change from having one's character dominated by one element and to having another element predominate – say transforming from a wood to a water personality. But, it is possible to use your yielding awareness skills to increase your understanding and have your personality become more in-tune with the characteristics of the other elements. This would lead to a more balanced expression of the elements within yourself. Still, this is not necessarily the goal. Sometimes you only need to embrace the positive characteristics of your dominant element and take advantage of how they will help you.

If, however, you become aware that a negative aspect of one of the elements is leading to problems, you can use your understanding of the Five Element / Phase theory to adopt practices, both physical and mental, that will help lessen the excesses and allow for more balance.

When it comes to relationships, the Five Element / Phase theory is useful in determining how best to relate to others in a way that yields positive results. For example, if one of another person's Fire element traits is an obstacle, you can seek to find a Fire element characteristic of that individual that you can resonate with and show that empathy in your words and actions by relating to that positive trait.

A basic understanding of this theory's use and application will enhance yielding awareness. But, first, it is helpful to know a bit of history regarding the Five Element / Phase theory origins.

Although several of the aspects found in the Five Element / Phase theory (such as the five directions) go back as far as 1766 BCE, the Five Element / Phase theory itself was not fully developed by Zou Yen until about 350 BCE. The Chinese have always used poetic images to describe the various components of the Five Element / Phase theory. Each descriptive image is rich in associative value.

Similarly, the explanation below also relies on poetic imagery to make its points.

For example, the Wood element is associated with the spring season because it grows rapidly during this time of year. The Fire element is associated with the summer season because of the increased heat during those months when the sun reaches its full zenith. The Earth element relates to the late summer season as the abundance of crops signifies the earth's many rewards. The Metal element is an expression of nature's rare and precious minerals and is associated with the fall season when much of nature's abundance returns to nourish the soil. And, lastly, the Water element is associated with winter because of its ability to freeze and adapt to the changing conditions of the season.

The Five Element / Phase model became an integral part of virtually every aspect of life in China. They are applied in areas as diverse as martial and meditative arts, architecture, painting, poetry, politics, medicine, and military strategy.

What follows is a discussion of the characteristics attributed to each of the five elements as they exist within human beings. Knowing the characteristics of various elements gives us a better understanding of ourselves and others. This Five Element / Phase theory information is intended as a guide that will increase your ability to apply yielding awareness to the many areas of your life.

Wood Element

Overall Characteristic

Wood is often associated with qualities such as growth, vitality, and strength, much like a tree that can withstand strong winds. Wood is also seen as flexible and adaptable, able to bend and change direction like bamboo. Spring is a time of growth, rebirth, and rapid expansion that shows the abundance of its power. Plant life surges to the surface rebounding from the long cold winter months. Excitement builds and the process of life awakens from the long dark lifeless days of winter. As the buds bloom and the trees come to life with leaves, this activity stirs the energy of all life. This change is expected yet it is unpredictable like the birth of a child whose precise arrival time is impossible to know. This anticipation leads to tension as well as the promise of release.

Wood Personality Traits

People who display characteristics of a Wood-dominated personality usually have many of these positive and negative traits:

- Seek challenges and push themselves
- Enjoy and do well under pressure
- Admire speed, novelty, and skill
- Embrace action, motion, and exploration with a passion
- Enjoy being the pioneer, excelling in your pursuits, and standing out as unique
- Frequently exhibit impatience and intolerance
- Possess eruptive emotions
- Can manifest as impulsivity or excessive discipline, as well as self-indulgence or self-punishing
- Can experience symptoms such as vascular headaches, muscle spasms, high blood pressure, nerve inflammations, and migratory pain
- Possibly susceptible to developing addictions to stimulants and sedatives

Physical Impact on the Body

The liver is the organ most closely associated with the Wood element. The liver instigates movement and inspires the mind by allowing tension and pressure to increase. As spring initiates the release of sap in the trees, so does the liver give rise to increased circulation of the blood and the building of Qi. By its collecting and releasing of blood, the liver effectively controls the intensity and strength of both actions. If you know you have many of these Wood characteristics, it is important to modulate your intensity and stay flexible. Learning to both retreat and yield, as well as surge forward while remaining calm, is important. Some of the basic Wood connections to the human body are:

- **Emotions:** Anger
- **Virtue:** Benevolence
- **Anatomy:** Tendons
- **Specific openings:** Eyes
- **Bowels:** Gall Bladder
- **Viscera:** Liver

Nature-Related Aspects

As noted, the Five Element / Phase theory is applicable to the external, natural world as well. Thus, the Wood element is said to apply to the following:

- **Directions:** East
- **Seasons:** Spring
- **Weather:** Wind
- **Developments:** Production
- **Colors:** Green
- **Tastes:** Sour
- **Sound:** Shout
- **Odor:** Rancid

Overall Personality Aspects

By understanding these connections to the Wood element, we can begin to be aware of what inspires the actions of a person with a Wood-dominant personality. In general terms, it can be said that they want to be in charge and miss the companionship of equals.

They yearn to do, to act, and can be subject to uncontrollable impulses. They like to both make and break the rules. They will demand freedom and are drawn to struggling. Often, they will feel invincible, but at the same time can fear vulnerability and loss of control.

Many of us are familiar with individuals who possess characteristics such as being bold, decisive, clear, and thriving under pressure. However, due to their ambitious nature, they may also tend to go to extremes, overexert themselves, and micromanage situations. For them, what was once a gratifying challenge can turn the corner and become an aggravating distress. It is then difficult for them to recover a balanced state. Moreover, their boldness can become aggressive and hostile, decisiveness can become impulsive and unyielding, and clarity can escalate into a fanatical adherence. When a person's Wood aspect is unrestrained, it can run wild, inflicting emotional trauma. If there is a desire to remain even-tempered and clear-minded, the person's muscles can tighten, and their attention focus can narrow too much. This will restrict their ability to increase and handle their energy, making them feel trapped and compressed.

Too strong of a Wood aspect has a detrimental impact on the body as well. When the liver Qi is exaggerated, inflated, or restricted it will express itself by a propensity toward tension headaches; a tendency to discharge pent-up energy in emotional outbursts: nervous erratic behavior like eating on the run, and inconsistent exercise. The person can develop intolerance, indulgence, obstinance, a strong body odor, a compulsion to overwork, and a need for sedatives to slow down.

A liver overburdened by too much of the Wood aspect has a negative impact on the Qi – collapsing, deflating, or exhausting it. Qi energy in this state gives rise to irritability, indecisiveness, sensitivity to noise, a loss of judgment and perspective, a need for stimulants, and feelings of being overwrought, overwhelmed, uptight, and fatigued. All of these reactions are linked to the deficiency and stagnation of the liver's Qi and blood. In times of deficiency or excess, the liver is unable to maintain the equanimity of a person's mind and emotions.

Fire Element

Overall Characteristic

All movement in our solar system and our life is oriented toward the sun, which is the ultimate embodiment of the Fire element. Even a microbe living at the bottom of the sea depends on the sun for its life and sustenance. The center of the solar system that gives life is the sun. In that sense, the sun is similar to the controlling influence of an emperor, president, CEO, or state leader.

Summer is the Fire element's season. Fire is dazzling, evaporating, trembling, interesting, exciting, and all-embracing. During summertime, the power of Fire is at its peak, and this is when plants and creatures reach their full potential. Summer is when we enjoy the fruits of our labor, try new experiences, and find fulfillment in newfound capacities. In the summer, Yang energy is dominant, with warmth, activity, and interaction at their peak. Fire, akin to the season of summer, is characterized by its expansiveness, brilliance, uninhibited nature, and warmth.

The heart, like the sun, is vital in sustaining life. It pumps the living fluid of the blood through the vessels, nourishing the body and mind with mindfulness. The heart and kidney are two distinct and unfathomable ends of the spectrum, creating a multifaceted display of our being. The Water element anchors one end, while the Fire element anchors the other, forming a construct that represents the interplay between these two elements.

Fire represents the individual and the inner space within which we cultivate and refine ourselves, whereas Water represents the universal and the surrounding space into which we flow and adapt. While water and its Yin energy are linked to our longevity, it is Fire that determines our breadth and scope. The Water element is like the seed and the root, whereas the Fire element yields the flower and the fruit. While Water is associated with the subconscious and the primal forces of nature, Fire symbolizes wakefulness and the development of wisdom and compassion.

As our self-awareness increases, the emergence of and the identification with the personal self is similar to the sun at its height during the summer solstice. Ancient sages stated that, when the Fire element in nature is at its peak, it illuminates the ten thousand manifestations of Dao in the world. The sun, however, is only at its peak for a brief moment in time. Once having reached the apex, the Yang energy begins to wane, and the influence of Yin energy begins to ascend.

> **The Virtue of Fire**
> "How is it that the heart corresponds to propriety?
> The heart is the essence of [the element] fire.
> [The quarter of fire is] the south, where the exalted yang holds a superior position, while the lowly yin holds an inferior position. Propriety maintains social differences between the exalted and the lowly. Therefore, the heart resembles fire, being red in color."
>
> — BAI HU DONG

If we know the characteristics of the Fire element and how it impacts our internal and external environment, we will better understand why people are the way they are.

Personality Traits

People who display characteristics of Fire personality usually will display the following traits.

- Enjoys excitement and finds pleasure in intimacy
- Intuitive and deeply empathetic with a strong sense of emotion
- Tends toward anxiety, agitation, and frenzy
- Can experience bizarre perceptions and sensations
- Enjoys warmth, liveliness, and energy
- Experiences nervous exhaustion and insomnia
- Suffers from palpitations, sweating, hypoglycemia, rashes, palsy
- Can abuse mind-altering substances
- Holds the belief in the potency of charm and aspiration
- Is fond of intense experiences, theatricality, and emotionalism

The Fire element's power comes from the ability to release heat and light and from seeking the joy in life and wanting to experience fulfillment. Fire-type personalities need to temper their emotions and contain their passions. Balance is an important goal such that Fire element people need to both conserve and share their resources, as well as learn when to withdraw and separate or, conversely embrace and merge.

Impact on the Body

Some of the basic Fire element impacts on the human body are the following:

- **Emotions:** Joy
- **Virtue:** Propriety
- **Anatomy:** Blood Vessels
- **Specific openings:** Tongue
- **Bowels:** Small Intestine
- **Viscera:** Heart

Nature-Related Aspects

The Fire element relates to the natural world and are said to apply as follows:

- **Directions:** South
- **Seasons:** Summer
- **Weather:** Hot
- **Developments:** Growth
- **Colors:** Red
- **Tastes:** Bitter
- **Sound:** Laugher
- **Odor:** Scorched

Overall Fire Personality Characteristics

As we start to understand the characteristics of the Fire element, we can begin to understand the inspirations behind a Fire-dominant personality's actions. To recognize the Fire personality, one must look past the exaggerated aspects to their true nature. They desire contact and intimacy but also need solitude. Individuals with a strong Fire element often love sensation and feeling, but at the same time, they may fear being overwhelmed by intensity. A Fire element person prefers to say yes and so has difficulty saying no. In many situations, they yearn for fusion and dread disintegration. They like to live in the moment and do not like to anticipate or plan for the future. They are often affectionate, open, expansive, generous, intuitive, warm, and bright.

There are negative aspects of the Fire-element personality. When they are overcome by their negative Fire tendencies, they tend toward heat, passion, dryness, redness, and excitability. If unrestrained, their Qi generates heat and agitation, which can produce mania, delusional behavior, and bizarre experiences like hallucinations, nightmares, and rushes of physical sensation. Their bodies can become flushed and feverish as they try to rid themselves of excess metabolic heat through sweating and radiation from the head, hands, and feet.

Fire-dominant personalities seek the thrill of imagined pleasures and feed on fantasy, sometimes generating unrealistic expectations of themselves and others. They will experience disappointment if the momentum that is created from unanchored exhilaration can result in disappointment when life does not measure up to their dreams. When this happens, it can be difficult for them to recover their buoyancy. This emotional pendulum, with its swings between the inflation of euphoria and the deflation of discouragement, can lead to them being frenzied or sad, in need of social interactions or isolated, talkative or passive, seductive or timid.

When their Qi is exhausted, they will become pale, subject to the cold, easily frightened, and confused. Sensitivity will turn to vulnerability, and intuition becomes enveloped with darkness and doubt. They are often withdrawn and ill-tempered dwelling on tales of longing and morbid images of suffering. This combination also leads to the hopeless romantic whose life can assume the self-pity-like qualities of a television melodrama.

When positive in nature, the Fire element gently supports life just as the fireplace warms the home. However, the Fire element can also manifest in a negative manner if it is deficient or excessive. When the sun does not shine for prolonged periods, cold and dampness fill the environment. Likewise, when the Fire element is deficient within, the cold takes over and the physiological processes begin to slow and contract. You may notice this by the slowing of the pulse, poor digestion reflecting the stomach's inability to "cook" food, lack of motivation, slower response times, and depression. This contraction presents a hurdle for maintaining relationships as well, if the personal Fire is withdrawn in an attempt to protect oneself, it will lead to disappointment.

In contrast, excessive Fire is like the sun parching the earth, creating an environment where life is a struggle for survival. Similarly, individuals with excess Fire may appear to be overly hot, their struggle for survival manifesting as an excessive need for control in every area of their life. Physically, excessive Fire may contribute to the acceleration of the physiological process, which may manifest as a quickened pulse, tendency to eat too quickly, or in activities done at a quickened or unhealthy rate, generating too much heat in the heart. The heart will often be overworked in an attempt to dissipate this heat, contributing to high blood pressure. When the heart and circulatory system is so expanded, this may lead to burnout in the form of a heart attack or stroke.

An excess of the Fire element can be found in the lack of boundaries in relationships. Moreover, the Fire element will burn significant others when it is perceived that they have crossed boundaries inappropriately.

Whether exaggerated or collapsed, excessive or diminished, Fire element personalities often experience a feeling of loss. The challenge for a Fire-dominant personality is to maintain a discrete identity without sacrificing their sensitivity and openness. Their virtue is their compassion, the capacity to know, feel, and understand what others are experiencing. This ability to show empathy can make them good communicators.

Earth Element

Overall Characteristic

The Earth is as massive as the Rocky Mountains, as gentle as a grassy meadow in the spring, inviting as the warm tropical waters of the Pacific, and as absorbing as a beautiful valley receiving rivers of sediment and rain. Existing across the continents, Earth holds countless territories and people of many cultures. In the sheltering hollows and crevices of the Earth's body, creatures sculpt terraces, fields, and pathways and gaze across marshes, forests, and open plains. The Earth is like a mother, nurturing all the life that depends on it.

During late summer, the Earth element is at its strongest, and it is an ideal time to support and nourish the digestive system. Eating locally grown, seasonal, and easily digestible foods can be beneficial. This is also a time to reflect on the abundance in our lives and to cultivate a sense of gratitude and generosity. In the body, the Earth element is associated with the spleen and stomach organs, which are responsible for extracting nutrients from food and distributing them throughout the body. Therefore, it is important to maintain a healthy diet and lifestyle during this time to support the digestive system and overall health.

Earth, its soil that feeds us and solid ground that gives us a place to call home, imparts stability. A tree is only as sturdy as the soil in which it is growing. A sapling that grows out of the gravel or sand is easily uprooted, but the tree that is able to send its roots deep into the soil or wrap them around the sturdy boulder stands strong, almost impossible to topple. When the Earth is too porous, the foundation holding us in place becomes unstable; Earth's density and mass sustain our momentum, keeping us aligned in the direction of our desired goal. But on the other hand, if Earth is too dense, things can become stunted, stuck, and unable to move in any direction.

Just as a spinning gyroscope keeps an aircraft flying on a focused path, the Earth generates the capacity for staying or changing direction without losing balance. The Earth serves as our primary reference point for center of gravity, around which all other facets of character align themselves. It forms the axis around which they revolve.

Unification and peacemaking are the guiding principles of the Earth-element person. The Earth-dominant individual uses their ability to create and maintain relationships to foster our interconnectedness with each other and the world. They concentrate on what is commonly shared and synthesize that which is separated into a unified and interdependent whole. As a peacemaker, the Earth person values serenity and stability, mediating conflict, converting it into harmony.

The Earth-element person is the master of positioning and leverage, able to alter his or her perspective, grasping what is central to achieving the most cooperation with the least sacrifice. The Earth person has a chameleon-like quality, able to adapt to and enhance the qualities of those around them. This ability puts others at ease and creates an atmosphere of trust.

The Earth element represents compassion and concern, serving as a compassionate advocate for those who need friendship, nourishment, and acknowledgement. The Earth-dominant personality works toward achieving harmony for the sake of harmony, tirelessly working to serve humanity as a great equalizer and mediator, preserving families and communities. It says, in a *Dao De Jing* chapter entitled "The Root of the Law-Holding the Singularity" that attaining the one (Dao) means having the following qualities and characteristics, while failure to attain the one has negative outcomes:

> "The skies attained the one and thus are clear,
> The earth attained the one and thus is tranquil,
> The spirit attained the one and thus is divine,
> The valley attained the one and thus is abundant,
> The myriad objects attained the one and thus live,
> The rulers attained the one and thus became the leaders of the world.
> These were all achieved from the one.
> The skies, without clarity, would break apart,
> The earth without tranquility would erupt,
> The spirit, without divinity, would dissipate,
> The valley, without abundance, would be barren,
> The myriad objects, without lives, would perish,
> The rulers, without leadership, would fall.
> Thus, those nobles use humility as their root, those with high ranks use the low position as their foundation.
> Therefore, those rulers called themselves alone, solitary, and unworthy.

Isn't this using the low to build their foundations? Isn't it?
What laymen despise are those who are alone, solitary and unworthy.
But those rulers use these as their titles.
Therefore, the ultimate honor is without honor,
Do not wish to be brilliant like jade but coarse like a rock."

— THE DAO DE JING, CHAPTER 39

Knowing the characteristics of the Earth element, and how it is connected to our internal and external environment, enhances our overall awareness gives us a better understanding of who and why we and others as we are.

Personality Aspects

People who display characteristics of Earth's personality usually will manifest these traits.

- Enjoy taking charge but prefer to avoid the spotlight
- Typically very agreeable and accommodating, as they strive to please others
- Desire harmony and unity
- Strong desire for loyalty, security, and predictability
- Tendency to worry, obsess, and have self-doubt
- Enjoy being involved and feeling needed
- Can be intrusive and overprotective.
- Tendency to become excessively stretched out and immobile.
- Present lethargy, indigestion, irregular or excessive appetite, water retention, and muscle tenderness (common symptoms of an imbalanced spleen)
- Hold unrealistic expectations and so suffer disappointment

Individuals with Earth-element characteristics possess immense power through their ability to foster, nourish, and maintain connections. However, to achieve balance, they must learn to balance their commitment to relationships with personal expression and solitude. This means developing self-reliance while also building community.

Physical Impact on the Body

The Spleen, like Indian summer, corresponds with the phase of Earth. Receiving and sharing solid and liquid, perceptions, and ideas, the spleen transforms food and experience into the substance of who we are.

- **Emotions:** Pensiveness
- **Virtue:** Integrity
- **Anatomy:** Muscles
- **Specific openings:** Mouth
- **Bowels:** Stomach
- **Viscera:** Spleen

Nature-Related Aspects

The Earth element is tied to the natural world in a number of ways, some of which are the following:

- **Directions:** Center
- **Seasons:** Late Summer
- **Weather:** Wet
- **Developments:** Transformation
- **Colors:** Yellow
- **Tastes:** Sweet
- **Sound:** Sing
- **Odor:** Sweet

Overall Earth Personality Aspects

As we explore the Earth element, we can gain insight into the motivations of individuals with an Earth-dominant personality. Such individuals often experience life's opposing forces. They may crave stillness, only to feel stagnant. They may desire fullness, but also feel weighed down and overwhelmed. They may seek emptiness while fearing a lack of substance. They may yearn for change while simultaneously wanting things to remain the same. And even though they enjoy being needed, they may also fear losing their identity and being consumed by others.

To recognize the Earth-element personality, look for someone who has a sociable, sunny disposition and who is supportive, pliant, reliable, and wise. Someone able to infuse balance, consistency, and focus on their extended network of relationships. They tend to have a way of inserting themselves into other people's affairs in a way that gains peoples' trust and appreciation. Like the earth itself, they are always there, permeating their social environment, offering assistance and aid whenever it is possible.

There are some drawbacks. An Earth-dominant personality will often become entangled in a web of details and complexity. They can overperform their role of intermediary and caretaker so that what was helpful becomes overbearing and inhibiting and what was nurturing becomes intrusive and overprotective. If the spleen's influence is too much, imbalance results. With the body tending toward absorption rather than conversion, density rather than action, a gathering of mass rather than energy. As a consequence, the Earth personality's gathered thoughts, feelings, fluids, and food settle and congeal rather than move and transform freely.

When the Earth personality's concern and involvement become worrisome burdens, the ability to bring things together is lost. Falling into gloom and despair, they will become engulfed by self-pity and dissatisfaction. They will have dramatic fluctuations in appetite, weight, and self-esteem that are a consequence of their loss of control. Their relaxed mannerisms take on a confusing quality and become scattered, lacking self-confidence and clarity. Sometimes they will become so consumed with what they should do that they will end up getting nothing done. Their overwhelming uncertainty defeats their attempts to rescue themselves or even ask for help.

Being called on to bring people together, the Earth person will spark them into action and rescue them in the same way an incoming tide frees a beached whale from the sand, returning them to a comfortable and secure existence. People who are Earth dominant are very social and it is important for them to maintain their social network for their own well-being as well as for their community.

Metal Element

Overall Characteristic

Metal is as austere as a parched plain before winter downpours, as sharp as a high mountain top cutting through the fog into an unmistakable empty sky. In the Five Element / Phase theory, the Metal phase embodies the power of restraint, separation, and refinement.

The autumn season is when things start to wither and decay. Trees shed their leaves as they start to decompose, returning to the soil just as the remains of crops are plowed under. The return of fruit and plant life to the soil fertilizes and enriches the soil for next year's growth. Life everywhere is starting to turn inward as tree sap retreats inward towards the roots. This is a time for eliminating the things we do not need and for gathering in what we need to survive the winter. Just as the plant life turns inward, so do the animals prepare for the slow winter months ahead.

The Metal element, associated with autumn, represents the refinement and purification of the self, just as metals are purified through fire and other processes. In traditional Chinese medicine, this element is connected to the lungs and large intestine, organs that are responsible for taking in and letting go, respectively. This is a time for letting go of what is no longer needed and for refining what remains.

In the natural world, autumn is a time of transformation and preparation. Leaves fall and decay, returning to the earth and providing nourishment for new growth in the future. The Metal element personality understands the importance of letting go and releasing what no longer serves them, in order to make room for growth and new beginnings.

Just as metal can be shaped and formed into different structures, the Metal element personality values order, structure, and discipline. They may also have a strong sense of aesthetics and appreciate beauty in simple, elegant forms.

Overall, the Metal element encourages us to let go of what no longer serves us, to refine and purify ourselves, and to embrace structure and order as a means of personal growth and transformation.

With autumn comes a sense of gathering in and storing that is mixed with a feeling of loss as the sun begins to fade and the cool air dominates the day. Yin energy grows and the Yang lessens. This is a season of dramatic change, but just as the spring was an expansive time of breaking through and proliferation, the fall is a contractive time of pulling in and dying back. The life cycle runs full circle in the autumn.

In this stage, the Dao represents the return from the height of self-awareness back to the return of the self, back to Dao. This transition is directed by the Metal element as the cycles of the seasons move from the bright light of the summer into the darkness of winter. Here we return to the fundamental core and, if we have fulfilled our destiny, our return occurs at a higher, more evolved level for our awareness having grown during another seasonal round of existence.

The Chinese character for Metal consists of a mine shaft covered by a roof holding two gold nuggets. Gold is the most valuable metal and therefore is considered to possess the qualities comprising the essence of the Metal element. In nature, minerals and metals play an essential role in providing the earth, plants, and all living beings with valuable nutrients and structural support. For example, metals like iron and magnesium are essential micronutrients that plants need for photosynthesis and growth. Similarly, minerals like calcium, phosphorus, and potassium are vital for maintaining the structure and health of the soil, which in turn supports the growth of plants and other organisms. Additionally, some minerals like quartz and mica contribute to the physical structure of the earth's crust, while others like copper and gold have been used for various purposes by humans throughout history.

The Metal element displays the qualities of hardness and strength. However, too much rigidity is problematic. Therefore, suppleness is an important quality for metal to possess. The Metal element's virtue is that it can be recast or remolded many times. Like water, the Metal element may take on any form, but unlike water, metal holds its form on its own. Metal is used to make weapons, and its ability to be honed to a fine edge enables it to cut to the core of things. Metal can be brilliant shining and inspirational in its many manifestations.

The Metal element is often difficult for Qigong students to understand and apply in relation to the human body. Physically, metal occurs within the minerals that nourish and give strength to the structure of our bones and tissue. When assessing the quality of a person's Metal element, it is important to draw on the imagery of the many ways metal is present in nature.

A strong indicator of a too dominant Metal personality is someone who is cold and piercing in their analysis and who remains fixed and unyielding in their perspective. Their attitude would resemble brittle metal – tarnished and cracking – lacking in a sense of self-worth. On the other hand, a well-balanced Metal personality might appear radiant like a diamond, inspiring others with their brilliance and obvious intrinsic value.

"The Dao of the Heaven,
    is it just like drawing a bow?
   The high is lowered,
   and the low is raised higher.
   Reduce what has excess,
   and add it to what is lacking.
   Take away from those who have excess,
   give to those who are lacking,
   The Dao of Heaven,
   always takes away from excess and gives it to those who are lacking.
   (However), the Dao of humans is not the same,
   take away from those who are lacking to give to those who already have excess.
   Who is able to offer his surplus to the world?
   Only those who have the Dao.
   Thus, sages do things without conceit,
   Achieve the goal by claiming no credit.
   They do not wish to display their superiority."

— THE DAO DE JING

Knowing the characteristics of Metal in the Five Element / Phase theory and how it is connected to our internal and external environment enables us to become more self-aware of ourselves and others.

Personality Aspects

People who have a Metal-dominant personality usually will display these traits. Specifically, they:

- Value morality, prudence, and those in positions of power.
- Typically, strive to live in accordance with logic and ethics
- Strive to maintain the highest standards for themselves and expect the same from others
- Hold great admiration for aesthetics, ritual, and elegance
- Exhibit a tendency toward aloofness and restraint
- May appear reserved, aloof, and rigid
- May experience physical symptoms such as stiff joints and muscles, dry skin and hair, shallow breathing, sensitivity to climate, and poor circulation
- Have an inclination toward definition, structure, and discipline
- They may display traits of self-righteousness and become disillusioned easily
- May exhibit tendencies toward being authoritarian, uncompromising, and meticulous

The Metal element personality draws strength from their ability to shape and refine, but may feel the need to balance their rationality, self-control, and meticulousness with more passion, spontaneity, and social involvement.

Physical Impact on the Body

The lungs are associated with the Metal element and correspond to the temperament of the season, they gather inward and refine the Qi sending it down to nourish the body with pure essence. Just as the skin serves as the body's outermost boundary, the lungs serve as a protective barrier against external threats and help maintain the body's internal balance. Some of the basic Metal connections to the human body and nature are:

- **Emotions:** Sorrow
- **Virtue:** Righteousness
- **Anatomy:** Skin and Hair
- **Specific openings:** Nose
- **Bowels:** Large Intestine
- **Viscera:** Lungs

Nature-Related Aspects

The Metal element is common in the natural world and relates to it in a variety of ways.

- **Directions:** West
- **Seasons:** Autumn/Fall
- **Weather:** Dry
- **Developments:** Harvest
- **Colors:** White
- **Tastes:** Spicy
- **Sound:** Weep
- **Odor:** Rotten

Overall Metal Personality Aspects

As we start to understand these connections to the Metal element, we can begin to understand what inspires the actions of a Metal-dominant personality. They want relationships but need distance. They know what is right and accept what is safe. They will often aspire towards beauty and settle for utility. They desire joy while fearing spontaneity. They will enjoy creativity, ingenuity, but can be intolerant of disorder and dissonance.

To recognize people with Metal attributes, notice how they will tend to express themselves by their sense of symmetry, self-discipline, purity of ideals, and logical mind. It is important for them that people fulfill their obligations and act equitably. They prefer things to have shape, sequence, and definition, and they are most comfortable in settings where they can determine how events will unfold.

As the Wood type was expansive and potentially chaotic, like a bull in a China shop, the Metal type is contractive and potentially rigid like a puffed-up military officer. When their tendencies become exaggerated, authoritarianism, perfectionism, and assertiveness replace flexibility, self-discipline, and critical thinking. Their single-minded focus on control causes inhibition of digestion, restricted breathing, a flattening of effect, and a blunting of their ability to sense and perceive.

The persistence of their negative aspects can trigger a collapse into internal disorder, a loss of personal values, and self-definition. Their inner resolve can disappear and be replaced by reliance on outer constraints. If they find themselves having difficulty adapting to changing circumstances or overwhelmed by disappointment and sorrow, they will tend to look for outside answers to resolve their internal doubts and grief.

All of this is ironic given that, generally, they are a model of rationality and self-control. Loss of both leaves them confused by internal forces and grasping at external rules to resolve that confusion. What was a fixation upon an inflexible set of standards and values, becomes a swamp of moral confusion and doubt. Having the tendency to personal cleanliness, household order, and careful expression can stand on its head as they collapse and surrender to sloppy dress, domestic disarray, and a mess of impulses that elude their control.

When the stability of the Metal-dominated personality is undermined, their need to differentiate and order things intensifies. Their need to be in control explains their devotion to correct behavior and thinking, as does their commitment to fixed distinctions between good and bad, right and wrong. When they are thwarted, peace becomes dullness, openness is suppressed, and order becomes ritualized routine.

Having "the courage of your convictions" describes the harmonious synthesis or resolution of the opposition between Metal and

Wood. In this context, Metal serves as the benchmark or gauge for moral principles, while Wood supplies the drive and vigor needed to manifest these principles in practice, which is to say, to demonstrate ethical conduct. The pair of Metal and Wood signifies a mutually beneficial interdependence of opposing yet complementary forces: Metal symbolizes restriction, limitation, and reduction, while Wood embodies expansion, growth, and stimulation. Together, they represent a balance of inhibition and excitation, restraint and striving, and reduction and proliferation. Whereas on the negative side, the Wood type can explode without a sign of ignition, the Metal personality will react by collapsing inward like a punctured balloon.

The polarity between Metal and Fire is clearly defined and complementary. Between them, they are tight and loose, analytic and intuitive, sensitive and sensual, distinct and merged. As Fire reveres passion and empathy, Metal esteems mindfulness and right action. When they are joined together, a kind mind with consideration often prevails. The combination of virtue and love describes the harmonious synthesis between Metal and Fire. Whereas the Fire-type becomes confused through excitement and euphoria, the Metal type becomes stuffy through suppression and boredom.

The Metal-dominant personality displays its characteristics by interacting easily with other people, feel inwardly secure, able to easily distinguish their own thoughts, feelings, and values from others. They will not feel vulnerable to outside influences and opinions, nor will they feel compelled to compose their standards or sensibilities on others. They are authentic to their inner selves, feeling secure and open to receiving, expressive and motivated, principled and confident.

Water Element

Overall Characteristic

Water can change its shape to discover the deepest of crevasses; it is as dark and fertile as the womb, as enduring as a crystal-clear tropical sea. Water ascends to fullness in the cold of winter when the trees and plants energetically return to their roots, animals thicken their fur, and lakes and streams turn to ice. Everything slows down and the energy is concentrated, pulled back to its center.

In this phase of apparent calm and inactivity, a concealed process of incubation and sprouting occurs beneath the surface. This time of hibernation allows new life to emerge by retreating to its core and seeking nourishment. Life's fundamental essence endures in its most rudimentary form, lying dormant until it blossoms once more in the springtime. As some animals hibernate, they could be mistaken for dead except for the subtle rising and falling of the breath and gentle warmth coming from within. During the winter, they leave the plentiful meadows, resting until the desire of hunger takes over as the spring signals the intense activity of a new cycle.

> "Virtue and Transformation: Fear into Wisdom
> How is it that the kidneys correspond to wisdom?
> The kidneys are the essence of the element water,
> and wisdom proceeds unceasingly without any doubt or uncertainty.
> Water likewise moves forward without uncertainty."
>
> — BAI HU DONG

Water is a symbol of the fundamental and primordial forces of human nature, as well as the domain of the collective and personal unconscious. It represents the ancient flow from which life forms materialize. Water connects the past and the future, ancestors and descendants, and is the source of our intuition and wisdom.

The manifestation of the first stage of movement of the Dao in the world is represented by the Water element. In assessing the qualities of each element within a human being, imagine how each element occurs in nature. For example, Water may occur as a single translucent droplet, a fresh cleansing rain promoting new life in the spring, a cool clear stream, a river overflowing its banks, a tidal wave overwhelming all that lies in its path, or as an entire ocean, deep, dark, and secretive. Using water in nature as an archetype, we can characterize the characteristics of the Water element metaphorically.

The environmental condition that changes the Water element is the cold. Therefore, sometimes individuals with a driving ambition may be described as "cold" if they allow their assertion of willpower, like a tidal wave, to overwhelm the natural development of others. Cold may also prevent us from manifesting our potential because the Water element freezes similar to the way ice floes prevent the flowing of a stream in winter, the season associated with the Water element. Water is associated with the wisdom that comes from experience and understanding. This wisdom is considered essential for navigating the ebb and flow of life, just as water is essential for sustaining life and flowing around obstacles in its path.

> "The reason that the rivers and seas be the lords of the hundreds of valleys,
> Is because they are adept at staying low,
> thus, they can be the lords of the hundred valleys.
> Therefore, those sages,
> who wish to be over people,
> must first speak humbly to them;
> who wish to lead people,
> must place themselves behind them.
> Thus, those sages, though they are positioned above people,

people do not feel burdened,
though situated in front, people do not feel harmed.
Consequentially, the people in the world are happy to push sages
forward without resentment.
Because they do not contend,
The world cannot contend with them."

— THE DAO DE JING

Once we know the characteristics of the Five Element / Phase's Water element and how it is connected to our internal and external environment, we can start to be aware of and understand, the information that we are given regarding those environments.

Personality Traits

People with a Water-dominant personality usually will display the following traits.

- Known for their eloquence, intelligence, and introspection
- Possess a sharp and penetrating intellect, with a tendency toward critical analysis and thorough scrutiny
- Prefers to maintain a mysterious and elusive persona, often concealing their true identity or intentions
- Tends to be solitary and may feel a sense of isolation and loneliness
- May lack tact, hold grudges, and exhibit mistrust toward others
- Water-element imbalance may include atherosclerosis (hardening of the arteries), deteriorating oral health (teeth and gums), back pain, feeling cold, and decreased libido

- Tendency to be self-contained and self-sufficient individuals
- Have a deep desire to gain knowledge and understanding
- Tendency to keep their emotions to themselves and may seem distant or unresponsive

Water personalities draw power from their capacity for creativity, intuition, and adaptability. However, they may need to balance their tendencies toward being cold, detached, and reserved with qualities such as warmth, empathy, and openness to fully tap into their potential. This requires them to take the risk of being vulnerable and making connections, embracing a softer side and allowing themselves to be open and exposed.

Physical Impacts on the Body

The kidneys can be seen as a symbol of a bear in hibernation in its cave, as they house the seed of life or essence that nourishes and revitalizes our life force.

- **Emotions:** Fear
- **Virtue:** Wisdom
- **Anatomy:** Bones
- **Specific openings:** Ears
- **Bowels:** Urinary Bladder
- **Viscera:** Kidneys

Nature-Related Aspects

Water constantly interacts with a number of aspects in the natural world:

- **Directions:** North
- **Seasons:** Winter

- **Weather:** Cold
- **Developments:** Storage
- **Colors:** Black
- **Tastes:** Salty
- **Sound:** Groan
- **Odor:** Putrid

Overall Water Personality Aspects

As we start to understand these connections to the Water element, we can begin to understand the inspirations behind the actions a person with a Water-dominant personality may display.

They are firmly rooted in themselves, tough, self-possessed, and distinguished to the point of being unconventional. Like an underground spring, they have deep reserves of strength that can be tapped into with some effort. If their tenacity, prudence, introspection, and solitary independence becomes exaggerated, they may appear hardened, crusty, cynical, arthritic, cold, and deadened as if fossilized. If they reach this point of freezing, they will crack like a sheet of ice. Their dissembling takes the form of fear, a constant premonition of extinction of their self through a loss of substance and will.

They become suspicious and stingy, worried that everyone wishes to appropriate their thoughts and feelings, their secrets, and their warmth. Without a live connection to other people, their grasp on reality outside themselves becomes fragile. When their vitality is diminished through prolonged isolation, the integral structure of their identity collapses. Their native sense of self, of continuity and future, that "I was born, I exist, I will survive," melts into the terror of invasion and absorption, of drowning in a vast, undifferentiated sea. What was tough and hard becomes porous and fragile: faith, desire, and motivation collapse. They succumb to asocial tendencies and escape into a self-imposed Siberian tundra. What was defined and emergent will become as infantile and primitive as a novel with only one word. Water takes the form of the vessel that contains it, so a Water-dominant personality cannot take shape without developing the expansive, actualizing aspects of his or her being. Water-element types have the propensity either to harden and compact into stone or lose form, becoming undefined, in a sense, anonymous.

As with all types, the Water element personality's strengths need to be balanced by connectedness to the Earth, to the warmth and expressiveness of Fire, to the action of Wood, and to the structure of Metal. Development of these aspects will enable them to enjoy the independence and creative gifts of their temperament.

Final Thoughts

The Five Phases are not static entities, but rather dynamic expressions of primal forces that exist within a universe of larger and smaller systems that interact and cogenerate, contract and expand. The relational continuum referred to as Yin and Yang is characterized by more concrete and palpable forms at one end and more abstract and indistinct forms at the other end. The five forces or elements follow a specific pattern as they move through different phases: Water represents consolidation and potentiation, Wood represents expansion and initiation, Fire represents completion and fulfillment, Metal represents contraction and release, and Earth represents stability and poise. These phases are present in the cosmos, as well as in every human being and process. Each person has a hidden core around which they revolve, and an external terrain that can be compared to the poles of Water and Fire, or the organs of the kidney and heart.

Rotational movement takes place within the dynamic interplay of opposing forces represented by Metal and Wood, as well as the corresponding organs of the lung and liver. Earth element is associated with the spleen, which is considered the axis of revolution and the center of gravity and mass. It is believed that the Earth element plays a crucial role in maintaining a state of harmonious tension among all other forces in the body and in the universe.

This energetic model depicts the dynamics of interaction, wherein the vital force pulsates, inhaling and exhaling, creating and breaking down, charging and discharging, and propelling the cyclical flow of life energy. Similar to the magnetic needle of a compass that perpetually points to north and south, Water invariably signifies the force that conserves, amasses, and generates energy, which later replenishes following discharge. On the other hand, Fire consistently represents the end point of expansion and culmination. Lines of correspondence between the energies of the five phases and individual structure and process established "character types."

Carl Jung formulated the concept of "archetypes" to elucidate the recurrent motifs that possess universal significance, harmonizing the insights derived from both psychoanalytic theory and Eastern mysticism. We have named five archetypes with human characteristics for each phase, inspired by Jung, in an effort to merge the principles of Western psychology with Chinese correspondence thinking. This single phase dominates, molding and characterizing us, while simultaneously providing the most significant framework for our growth and development to unfold.

The symbolic figures linked to each phase embody the central issues and questions that are relevant to our lives. Describing someone as a Pioneer, Philosopher, Peacemaker, Alchemist, or Wizard conveys an image of the most empowering environment in which a person can realize their potential for self-expression. The Wood element is exemplified by the Pioneer, who embodies an action-oriented spirit, fearlessly venturing into the unknown and facing obstacles head-on. They possess a bold and adventurous nature, always seeking new discoveries and overcoming resistance. Whereas the Philosopher, who characterizes Water, is preoccupied with seeking what is real and investigating the undisclosed mysteries through his own creative mind. The Peacemaker, stable, centered, and relaxed personifies Earth, drawn toward being a mediator in the service of harmony and unity. The Wizard, who embodies Fire, exudes charisma and enthusiasm, instilling confidence that aspirations can be actualized and yearnings can be gratified. Meanwhile, the Alchemist, who represents Metal, examines, scrutinizes, and dissects phenomena to extract underlying laws and principles that serve the cause of universal harmony.

By coming to know the five elements and their various relationships to nature and human actions, you begin to notice patterns and start to see things that may go unobserved by others. Remember, that the Five Element / Phase theory is a guide and that people sometimes will have characteristics of more than one element. Also, be aware that external forces can stimulate reactions outside of someone's normal inherent response as characterized by their element. For example, a person who is a Wood-element dominant personality will respond differently to a physical confrontation in the fall season than they would in the middle of springtime. Knowing this leads us to the multitude of applications of how we can apply this understanding into our daily lives.

Let's look at one more idea here on how we can use this to our advantage. Suppose you are a grade-school teacher and know that children will be less likely to be rambunctious in the fall and winter seasons. Knowing this, you could adjust the curriculum that typically sparks mischievous antics that it takes place during fall and winter season. And, similarly, save the lessons that do not spur the same antics for the springtime. This will naturally help balance the rhythm of the class and help to keep the children more focused.

This appendix barely touches on the idea of the Five Element / Phase theory. This theory is useful in any life situation. You do not need to master this concept but, with a small amount of study, it will improve your internal and external awareness and give you a hand up in all three areas of yielding: physical, mental, and emotional. At the height of self-awareness, it is possible to catch a glimpse of our original self that has been lost. At this moment, we could seek to transcend the personal self and return to the universal self. This realization or surrender is often the first step in restoring our original nature.

RESOURCES

1. Harriet Beinfield and Efrem Korngold, *Between Heaven and Earth* (New York: Random House, 1991).
2. Rhonda Bryne, *The Secret* (New York: Atria Books, 2018).
3. Jim Collins, *Good to Great* (New York: Harper Business, 2001).
4. Jack Cranfield and D. D. Watkins, *Key to Living the Law of Attraction* (Deerfield Beach, FL: Health Communications, 2007).
5. Jack Cranfield and Pamela Bruner, *Tapping into Ultimate Success* (Carlsbad, CA: Hay House, 2012).
6. Jack Canfield, Mark Hanson, Jeanna Gabellini, and Eva Gregory, *Mastering the Law of Attraction*, Cos Cob, CT: Backlist, a unit of Chicken Soup for the Soul Publishing, 2012).
7. Jack Canfield, *The Success Principles* (New York: William Morrow, 2015).
8. Jan Diepersloot, *The Tao of Yichuan* (Walnut Creek, CA: Center for Healing and the Arts, 1999).
9. Larry Donnithorne, *The West Point Way of Leadership* (New York: Currency Doubleday, 1993).
10. Malcolm Gladwell, *Blink* (New York: Little, Brown and Company, 2005).
11. Robert Greene, *The 33 Strategies of War* (New York: Penguin Books, 2006).
12. Esther Hicks and Jerry Hicks, *The Law of Attraction* (Carlsbad, CA: Hay House, 2006).
13. Lonny Jarrett, *Nourishing Destiny* (Stockbridge, MA: Spirit Path Press, 2009).
14. Genie Laborde, *Influencing with Integrity* (Palo Alto, CA: Syntony Publishing, 1984).
15. John Little, *Jeet Kune Do* (Boston: Charles E. Tuttle, 1997).
16. John Little, *The Warrior Within* (New York: McGraw-Hill, 1996).

17. Robert Moonkin, *Bargaining with the Devil* (New York: Simon and Schuster, 2010).
18. George Thompson and Jerry Jenkins, *Verbal Judo* (New York: HarperCollins, 2013).
19. Chogyam Trungpa, *Cutting Through Spiritual Materialism* (Boulder: Shambhala, 1973).
20. Jou Tsung Hwa, *The Tao of Meditation* (Scottsdale: Tai Chi Foundation, 2000).
21. Gary Vaynerchuk, *Jab, Jab, Jab, Right Hook* (New York: HarperCollins, 2013).
22. Chris Voss and Tahl Raz, *Never Split the Difference* (New York: HarperCollins, 2016).
23. Josh Waitzkin, *The Art of Learning* (New York: Free Press, 2007).
24. Jwing-Ming Yang, *The Dao in Action* (Wolfeboro NH: YMAA Publication Center, 2019).
25. Jwing-Ming Yang, *The Root of Chinese Chi Kung* (Jamaica Plain, MA: YMAA Publication Center, 1989).
26. Jwing-Ming Yang, *Tai Chi Theory and Martial Power* (Jamaica Plain, MA: YMAA Publication Center, 1996).
27. Jwing-Ming Yang, *Qigong Meditation* (Boston, MA: YMAA Publication Center, 2006).
28. Jwing-Ming Yang, *The Dao De Jing* (Wolfeboro, NH: YMAA Publication Center, 2018).
29. Jwing-Ming Yang, *Tai Chi Chuan Martial Applications* (Jamaica Plain, MA: YMAA Publication Center, 1986).
30. Shou Yu Liang and Wen-Ching Wu, *Qigong Empowerment* (Providence, RI: Way of the Dragon Publishing, 1997).

ACKNOWLEDGMENTS

I would like to take a moment to express my heartfelt gratitude to the individuals who have played a significant role in the creation and publication of *The Yielding Warrior*. Their unwavering support, guidance, and encouragement have been instrumental throughout this writing journey.

First and foremost, I am deeply grateful to my family for their endless love and understanding. Your unwavering belief in me and the sacrifices you made to provide me with the time and space to write are beyond measure. Your constant support has been a source of strength and inspiration.

To my students, thank you for being the driving force behind this book. Your dedication, curiosity, and eagerness to learn fueled my own passion for the subject matter. Witnessing your growth and transformation on the mat has been a profound source of motivation and has greatly influenced the content within these pages.

I am indebted to my teachers, whose wisdom and expertise shaped my understanding of the meditative arts. Your guidance and willingness to share your knowledge have been invaluable. Your commitment to passing down the teachings of this ancient practice paved the way for my own exploration and discoveries.

I would like to extend a special thank you to Susan Stoner, my exceptional mentor throughout this writing process. Your expertise in the field of literature and your unwavering support have been instrumental in shaping this book into its final form. Your insightful feedback, constructive criticism, and words of encouragement have been pivotal in refining my ideas and bringing clarity to my writing.

Finally, I would like to express my gratitude to all those who have supported me in various ways, whether through beta reading, offering encouragement, or simply being there to listen. Your contributions have made a significant impact, and I am truly grateful for your presence in my life.

To everyone mentioned here and to those whose names I may have inadvertently omitted, thank you from the depths of my heart. Your unwavering belief in me and your role in shaping *The Yielding Warrior* is deeply appreciated.

ABOUT THE AUTHOR

Jeff Patterson is a highly experienced martial artist, residing in Portland, Oregon, with over thirty-six years of practice under his belt. He is renowned for his exceptional skills in Brazilian Jiu-Jitsu, Eskrima, Tai Chi, Qigong, Muay Thai, and Kenpo, having achieved black belt equivalency in all these martial arts disciplines.

Jeff's passion for martial arts and its transformative power led him to establish Northwest Fighting Arts and Portland Tai Chi Academy, an organization that has flourished over the past twenty-nine years, with over twenty-five thousand students benefiting from his teachings. With a large student base of over five hundred individuals, the academy offers a diverse range of classes and meticulously crafted comprehensive curricula for each martial art they teach, including Muay Thai, Western Boxing, Jeet Kune Do, Filipino Arts, Brazilian Jiu-Jitsu, Tai Chi, and Qigong.

Jeff is a firm believer in the benefits of meditative arts and their power to enhance overall life experiences. He has extensively studied the historical, philosophical, and health aspects of meditative arts and recognized the importance of the yielding concept to attain expertise in each discipline. Through his dedication and teachings, he has witnessed positive and profound changes in his students, which fuels his ongoing passion for sharing his knowledge.

Before establishing his martial arts academy, Jeff served in the Marine Corps for four years and earned two bachelor's degrees in business from Portland State University. Utilizing his martial arts skills and teaching abilities, Jeff supported himself financially during his studies while continually expanding his knowledge by training with various instructors.

Jeff's expertise in Muay Thai stems from his long-term instructor Ajarn Chai Sirisute, a pioneer who introduced the art to the United States. Under Ajarn Chai's guidance, Jeff has trained for over thirty years and has witnessed the popularization of Muay Thai globally through his teacher's seminars and teachings. He has also trained extensively in Western Boxing, Filipino Arts, and Jeet Kune Do concepts under the mentorship of Punong Guro Leonard Trigg, who has produced Olympic and Professional champion fighters in Western Boxing.

Jeff's training in Brazilian Jiu-Jitsu includes studying under renowned masters such as Master Rigan Machado since 1992, who awarded him his Black Belt in 2007. He has also trained with other influential instructors such as Pedro Sauer, Rickson Gracie, Anibol Lobo, and Fabio Santos.

Jeff has a profound appreciation for Tai Chi and has studied under esteemed masters such as Sifu Leonard Trigg, Dr. Yang Jwing-Ming, Sifu Gregory Fong, and Sifu Thomas Flannel. However, his most significant influence in Tai Chi training comes from Grandmaster Sam Tam. Jeff has dedicated years to perfecting and refining his Tai Chi forms, encompassing various styles and weapons, under Grandmaster Sam Tam's guidance since 2004.

Jeff has authored three books, created two audio courses, and produced hundreds of instructional videos, sharing his extensive knowledge and expertise. Through his dedication and teachings, Jeff has positively impacted the lives of thousands of individuals, providing them with the tools and techniques to improve their overall well-being.

In conclusion, Jeff Patterson's vast experience, dedication, and passion for martial arts have led to the establishment of a successful organization benefiting thousands of individuals. His profound understanding of meditative arts and the yielding concept has enhanced his teachings, enabling his students to achieve mastery in their chosen discipline. Jeff's teachings continue to impact the lives of individuals globally, providing them with the tools to achieve greater physical and mental well-being.

THANK YOU

Congratulations on completing *The Yielding Warrior*! Your journey toward transformation and unlocking your true potential has just begun, and I am thrilled to be a part of it. Your dedication to personal growth is inspiring, and I am here to provide support every step of the way.

I invite you to visit our website at https://portlandtaichiacademy.com/online-training/ to explore our online program. This specially designed program incorporates many of the methods discussed in the book, offering you practical tools and guidance to deepen your practice. Whether you are new to meditative arts or already have experience, our program is tailored to meet you at your current level and guide you toward profound growth.

Additionally, I encourage you to sign up for our free email series, which provides valuable resources and insights to support you on your transformative journey. These tools will complement your practice and assist you in overcoming challenges along the way.

Having dedicated over thirty years to the meditative arts, I have witnessed countless individuals undergo life-altering transformations through consistent practice. By committing just twenty minutes a day to the practice for one year, you will experience an array of benefits that will undoubtedly inspire you to continue this lifelong journey.

Remember, the path to personal growth is a continuous one, and I am honored to accompany you on this incredible adventure. Should you have any questions or require further assistance, please don't hesitate to reach out.